We hope this book has been informative and helpful on your journey to understanding and celebrating older adults. Thank you for your interest and support!

Title: Forging New Frontiers: PoW's Impact on the Digital Economy

Subtitle: Unveiling the Transformative Influence of PoW Coins on Global Finance

Series: Trailblazers of the Blockchain: Unleashing the Power of PoW

By Alexander C. Blair

Table of Contents

Introduction...6

Exploring the Continued Evolution of PoW Coins 6

Introducing Book 3: Uncovering the Impact of Ixcoin, Freicoin, Dogecoin, Vertcoin, and SiaCoin.......................11

Understanding the Unique Contributions of Each Coin . 15

Chapter 1: Ixcoin (IXC), established 2011 - "Global decentralized currency." 19

Unveiling Ixcoin as a Global Decentralized Currency 19

The Genesis and Development of Ixcoin 23

Adoption and Community Engagement............................ 27

Evaluating Ixcoin's Role in the Cryptocurrency Ecosystem 32

Chapter 2: Freicoin (FRC), established 2012 - "Demurrage currency with distribution mechanisms.".. 37

Understanding Freicoin's Demurrage Currency with Distribution Mechanisms 37

Exploring the Concept of Demurrage and Its Purpose ... 42

Use Cases and Adoption in Economic Systems 47

Challenges and Future Prospects of Freicoin 51

Chapter 3: Dogecoin (DOGE), established 2013 - "The fun and friendly internet currency." 56

From Meme to Mainstream: The Journey of Dogecoin.. 56

The Fun and Friendly Internet Currency 60

Community-driven Initiatives and Philanthropy 64

Dogecoin's Cultural Impact and Future Potential 68

Chapter 4: Vertcoin (VTC), established 2014 - "Peer-to-peer digital currency with ASIC resistance."..... 72

Peer-to-Peer Digital Currency with ASIC Resistance 72

The Need for ASIC Resistance and Decentralization 76

Vertcoin's Commitment to Fair Mining and Security 80

Adoption and Use Cases in the Crypto Landscape 84

Chapter 5: SiaCoin (SC), established 2015 - "Decentralized cloud storage platform." **88**

Decentralized Cloud Storage Platform 88

Exploring Sia's Blockchain-based Storage Solution 92

Security, Privacy, and Cost Efficiency Advantages 96

Real-world Applications and Future Development 100

Chapter 6: Comparative Analysis and Synergies . 104

Contrasting the Unique Characteristics of the Featured Coins 104

Identifying Synergies and Potential Collaborations 110

Examining the Broader Impact of PoW Coins in the Crypto Industry 114

Chapter 7: Shaping the Future of Blockchain **118**

Evaluating the Role of PoW Coins in the Advancement of Blockchain Technology 118

Emerging Trends and Innovations..............................123

Speculating on the Future of PoW Coins and Their Impact on the Digital Economy 129

Conclusion **133**

Reflecting on the Contributions of PoW Coins Explored in Book 3 133

Summarizing the Key Takeaways and Lessons Learned 138

Looking Towards the Future: Opportunities and Challenges in the Blockchain Space 143

Key Terms and Definitions **148**

Supporting Materials..**152**

Introduction

Exploring the Continued Evolution of PoW Coins

In the ever-evolving landscape of cryptocurrencies, Proof-of-Work (PoW) coins have played a pivotal role in shaping the blockchain industry. These coins, which emerged as trailblazers after the rise of Bitcoin, have made groundbreaking contributions to the realm of digital finance. In this book, "Trailblazers of the Blockchain: Unleashing the Power of PoW," we embark on a captivating journey through the early blockchain era, delving into the untold stories of pure PoW coins and their impact on the digital economy.

Chapter 1: Ixcoin (IXC), established 2011 - "Global decentralized currency."

The genesis of Ixcoin marked an important milestone in the history of PoW coins. As an early player in the cryptocurrency ecosystem, Ixcoin aimed to establish itself as a global decentralized currency. In this chapter, we unveil the vision behind Ixcoin and its development from its inception to its current state. We explore the challenges faced by the Ixcoin community and the innovative solutions they employed to promote adoption and community engagement. By evaluating Ixcoin's role in the broader cryptocurrency ecosystem, we gain a deeper understanding of its unique contributions.

Chapter 2: Freicoin (FRC), established 2012 - "Demurrage currency with distribution mechanisms."

Freicoin introduced a novel concept to the world of cryptocurrencies: demurrage currency with distribution mechanisms. This chapter delves into the intricate details of Freicoin's economic model and explores the purpose of demurrage within a digital currency system. We examine the various use cases and adoption of Freicoin in economic systems, shedding light on the challenges it encountered along the way. Moreover, we discuss the future prospects of Freicoin and its potential impact on the digital economy.

Chapter 3: Dogecoin (DOGE), established 2013 - "The fun and friendly internet currency."

From its humble beginnings as a meme-based cryptocurrency, Dogecoin quickly gained popularity and became a significant player in the crypto space. This chapter takes us through the journey of Dogecoin, exploring its transformation from a fun and friendly internet currency to a widely recognized digital asset. We examine the community-driven initiatives and philanthropic endeavors that propelled Dogecoin into the spotlight. Furthermore, we analyze the cultural impact of Dogecoin and its potential for future growth.

Chapter 4: Vertcoin (VTC), established 2014 - "Peer-to-peer digital currency with ASIC resistance."

The emergence of Vertcoin brought attention to the importance of ASIC resistance and decentralization in the world of cryptocurrencies. In this chapter, we delve into the peer-to-peer nature of Vertcoin and its commitment to fair mining practices and security. We examine the adoption and use cases of Vertcoin within the crypto landscape, showcasing its role as a pioneer in promoting decentralized mining. By exploring Vertcoin's ASIC-resistant architecture, we gain insights into its impact on the broader blockchain ecosystem.

Chapter 5: SiaCoin (SC), established 2015 - "Decentralized cloud storage platform."

As the demand for secure and cost-efficient cloud storage solutions grew, SiaCoin emerged as a decentralized blockchain-based storage platform. This chapter explores the innovative features of Sia's storage solution and its advantages in terms of security, privacy, and cost efficiency. We examine real-world applications of SiaCoin and its potential to disrupt traditional cloud storage providers. Furthermore, we discuss the future development and potential challenges that SiaCoin may encounter.

Chapter 6: Comparative Analysis and Synergies

In this chapter, we conduct a comparative analysis of the unique characteristics of the featured PoW coins. By contrasting their attributes, we gain a deeper understanding of the diverse approaches within the PoW ecosystem. Additionally, we explore potential synergies and collaborations among these coins, identifying areas where they can complement each other's strengths and drive innovation in the blockchain industry.

Chapter 7: Shaping the Future of Blockchain

As PoW coins continue to evolve, their impact on the advancement of blockchain technology becomes increasingly significant. In this chapter, we evaluate the role of PoW coins in shaping the future of blockchain and the digital economy. We discuss emerging trends and innovations within the PoW space, envisioning the potential developments that may drive the industry forward. By speculating on the future of PoW coins, we explore their potential impact on financial systems, privacy, security, and the broader digital economy.

Conclusion

In this final chapter, we reflect on the contributions of the PoW coins explored in this book. We summarize the key takeaways and lessons learned from their evolution, triumphs, and challenges. By understanding the unique characteristics and potential collaborations among PoW coins, readers gain valuable insights into the past, present, and future of the blockchain industry. Ultimately, "Trailblazers of the Blockchain: Unleashing the Power of PoW" invites readers to join us on an exhilarating exploration of the pioneers of PoW coins as they forge a path towards a decentralized future in the digital economy.

Introducing Book 3: Uncovering the Impact of Ixcoin, Freicoin, Dogecoin, Vertcoin, and SiaCoin

Welcome to Book 3 of our series, "Trailblazers of the Blockchain: Unleashing the Power of PoW." In this installment, we delve into the untold stories and unique contributions of five remarkable Proof-of-Work (PoW) coins: Ixcoin, Freicoin, Dogecoin, Vertcoin, and SiaCoin. Each of these coins played a pivotal role in shaping the blockchain industry and has left a lasting impact on the digital economy. Join us as we explore the genesis, development, challenges, and triumphs of these pioneering cryptocurrencies.

Chapter 1: Ixcoin (IXC), established 2011 - "Global decentralized currency."

In this chapter, we embark on a journey to unveil the story behind Ixcoin, an early player in the cryptocurrency ecosystem. Ixcoin aimed to establish itself as a global decentralized currency, carving a path for financial sovereignty. We delve into the genesis of Ixcoin, tracing its development from its inception to its current state. Through an exploration of the challenges faced by the Ixcoin community and their innovative solutions, we gain insights into the broader impact of this trailblazing coin.

Chapter 2: Freicoin (FRC), established 2012 - "Demurrage currency with distribution mechanisms."

Freicoin introduced a revolutionary concept to the world of cryptocurrencies: a demurrage currency with distribution mechanisms. In this chapter, we dive deep into the intricate workings of Freicoin's economic model. We explore the purpose of demurrage within a digital currency system and its potential to address economic inequality. Through a detailed analysis of the use cases and adoption of Freicoin in economic systems, we gain a comprehensive understanding of its impact on the digital economy.

Chapter 3: Dogecoin (DOGE), established 2013 - "The fun and friendly internet currency."

From its origins as a lighthearted meme, Dogecoin quickly rose to prominence as a beloved and influential cryptocurrency. In this chapter, we uncover the journey of Dogecoin, exploring how it transitioned from a fun and friendly internet currency to a force to be reckoned with in the crypto space. We delve into the community-driven initiatives and philanthropic endeavors that propelled Dogecoin to the forefront. Moreover, we examine the cultural impact of Dogecoin and its potential to shape the future of digital finance.

Chapter 4: Vertcoin (VTC), established 2014 - "Peer-to-peer digital currency with ASIC resistance."

Vertcoin emerged as a pioneer in the fight against centralized mining and the importance of ASIC resistance. In this chapter, we explore the unique features of Vertcoin as a peer-to-peer digital currency. We delve into the reasons behind its commitment to fair mining practices and its emphasis on decentralization. By analyzing the adoption and use cases of Vertcoin within the crypto landscape, we gain insights into its impact on promoting a more democratic and secure blockchain ecosystem.

Chapter 5: SiaCoin (SC), established 2015 - "Decentralized cloud storage platform."

As the demand for secure and cost-efficient cloud storage solutions grew, SiaCoin stepped onto the stage as a decentralized blockchain-based storage platform. In this chapter, we unravel the intricacies of SiaCoin's decentralized cloud storage solution. We explore its advantages in terms of security, privacy, and cost efficiency. Through a thorough examination of real-world applications and the future development of SiaCoin, we gain a comprehensive understanding of its potential impact on revolutionizing cloud storage.

Conclusion

In this concluding chapter of Book 3, we reflect on the impact of Ixcoin, Freicoin, Dogecoin, Vertcoin, and SiaCoin.

Through our exploration of these groundbreaking PoW coins, we have witnessed their triumphs, challenges, and breakthroughs. By uncovering their unique contributions to the blockchain industry, we gain valuable insights into the past, present, and future of digital finance. Join us as we continue to forge new frontiers in the PoW landscape, forever changing the realm of digital finance.

Understanding the Unique Contributions of Each Coin

In Book 3 of our series, "Trailblazers of the Blockchain: Unleashing the Power of PoW," we embark on a journey to uncover the unique contributions of five exceptional Proof-of-Work (PoW) coins: Ixcoin, Freicoin, Dogecoin, Vertcoin, and SiaCoin. These coins have left an indelible mark on the blockchain industry, each bringing something distinct and valuable to the table. In this section, we will delve into the intricate details of their contributions, exploring how they have shaped the digital economy.

Chapter 1: Ixcoin (IXC), established 2011 - "Global decentralized currency."

Ixcoin, an early player in the cryptocurrency landscape, introduced the concept of a global decentralized currency. In this chapter, we examine Ixcoin's journey and its impact on the digital economy. We explore the genesis of Ixcoin, shedding light on its mission to provide financial sovereignty and empower individuals globally. By evaluating its role in promoting decentralization, transactional efficiency, and trust, we gain a comprehensive understanding of Ixcoin's unique contributions.

Chapter 2: Freicoin (FRC), established 2012 - "Demurrage currency with distribution mechanisms."

Freicoin revolutionized the cryptocurrency space with its demurrage currency model and innovative distribution mechanisms. In this chapter, we delve into the intricacies of Freicoin's economic system and its impact on the digital economy. We explore the purpose of demurrage, its potential to address economic inequality, and its unique characteristics as a currency with built-in incentives for circulation. By analyzing the use cases and adoption of Freicoin, we gain insights into its contributions to the broader blockchain ecosystem.

Chapter 3: Dogecoin (DOGE), established 2013 - "The fun and friendly internet currency."

Dogecoin, born out of an internet meme, captured the hearts of many and brought a unique spirit to the world of cryptocurrencies. In this chapter, we uncover the cultural impact and distinctive contributions of Dogecoin. We explore its journey from a fun and friendly internet currency to a philanthropic force, fostering community-driven initiatives and promoting social good. By examining its vibrant community, innovative marketing, and potential for mainstream adoption, we gain a deeper understanding of Dogecoin's remarkable contributions.

Chapter 4: Vertcoin (VTC), established 2014 - "Peer-to-peer digital currency with ASIC resistance."

Vertcoin emerged as a pioneer in promoting fair mining practices and combating centralization through ASIC resistance. In this chapter, we explore Vertcoin's unique contributions as a peer-to-peer digital currency. We delve into its commitment to decentralization, fair mining, and security. By analyzing its role in fostering a more inclusive and democratic blockchain ecosystem, we gain insights into Vertcoin's impact on the digital economy.

Chapter 5: SiaCoin (SC), established 2015 - "Decentralized cloud storage platform."

SiaCoin introduced a decentralized blockchain-based storage platform, revolutionizing the cloud storage industry. In this chapter, we unravel the unique contributions of SiaCoin and its impact on the digital economy. We delve into its secure and cost-efficient storage solutions, highlighting its advantages in terms of privacy, data integrity, and affordability. By examining its real-world applications, adoption, and future development, we gain a comprehensive understanding of SiaCoin's contributions to the blockchain ecosystem.

Conclusion

In this concluding chapter, we reflect on the unique contributions of Ixcoin, Freicoin, Dogecoin, Vertcoin, and SiaCoin to the digital economy. Each coin has brought its own set of innovative ideas, values, and functionalities, shaping the blockchain industry in distinct ways. By understanding their contributions, we gain valuable insights into the evolution of digital finance and the potential for future advancements. Join us as we continue to forge new frontiers in the world of PoW coins, unraveling the transformative power they hold in the decentralized digital economy.

Chapter 1: Ixcoin (IXC), established 2011 - "Global decentralized currency."

Unveiling Ixcoin as a Global Decentralized Currency

In this chapter, we delve into the fascinating story of Ixcoin, an early player in the cryptocurrency ecosystem that aimed to establish itself as a global decentralized currency. We explore the vision, mission, and unique characteristics of Ixcoin, shedding light on its role in shaping the digital economy. Join us as we unveil the story behind Ixcoin's journey and its impact on the blockchain industry.

1. The Genesis of Ixcoin:

1.1 Early Beginnings: We start by exploring the early beginnings of Ixcoin, tracing its roots back to its launch in 2011. We delve into the motivations and inspirations behind its creation, understanding the driving forces that led to the birth of this innovative cryptocurrency.

1.2 Principles and Objectives: Ixcoin was driven by a set of core principles and objectives. We delve into the key tenets that shaped Ixcoin's foundation, such as decentralization, transparency, and financial sovereignty. By understanding these principles, we gain insights into Ixcoin's unique approach to becoming a global decentralized currency.

2. The Development of Ixcoin:

2.1 Technical Features and Innovations: Ixcoin introduced several technical features and innovations that set it apart in the cryptocurrency landscape. We explore its underlying blockchain technology, consensus mechanisms, and the role of mining in securing the network. Additionally, we examine any notable upgrades or advancements that occurred throughout its development.

2.2 Governance and Decision-Making: Ixcoin's governance and decision-making processes played a crucial role in shaping its trajectory. We delve into the governance model adopted by Ixcoin, analyzing how decisions were made, and the involvement of the community in shaping the currency's future.

3. Adoption and Community Engagement:

3.1 Early Adoption and Growth: We analyze the early stages of Ixcoin's adoption, examining the factors that influenced its growth and expansion. We explore the challenges faced and milestones achieved during its journey towards becoming a recognized cryptocurrency.

3.2 Community Dynamics: The Ixcoin community played an essential role in its success. We dive into the dynamics of the community, exploring the contributions of developers, miners, users, and enthusiasts. We also highlight any notable community-driven initiatives or collaborations that emerged within the Ixcoin ecosystem.

4. Evaluating Ixcoin's Role in the Cryptocurrency Ecosystem:

4.1 Impact on Decentralization: Ixcoin aimed to promote decentralization in the cryptocurrency ecosystem. We evaluate its impact on decentralization, examining how it contributed to the broader movement towards a more distributed and democratic financial system.

4.2 Use Cases and Adoption: We explore the use cases and adoption of Ixcoin in real-world applications. This includes analyzing its role as a medium of exchange, store of value, and potential integration within various industries or sectors.

4.3 Challenges and Lessons Learned: No journey is without its challenges. We reflect on the obstacles faced by Ixcoin and the lessons learned from these experiences. By understanding the challenges encountered and the subsequent adaptations made, we gain insights into the resilience and adaptability of Ixcoin as a global decentralized currency.

Conclusion:

In this concluding section of Chapter 1, we reflect on the unveiling of Ixcoin as a global decentralized currency. We summarize the key insights gained from exploring its genesis, development, adoption, and impact. By understanding the unique characteristics and contributions of Ixcoin, we gain a deeper appreciation for its role in shaping the digital economy and paving the way for decentralized financial systems.

The Genesis and Development of Ixcoin

In this chapter, we delve into the intriguing genesis and development of Ixcoin, an early cryptocurrency that aimed to establish itself as a global decentralized currency. We explore the origins, motivations, and key milestones that shaped Ixcoin's journey. Join us as we uncover the fascinating story behind Ixcoin's creation and its subsequent development in the cryptocurrency landscape.

1. The Birth of Ixcoin:

1.1 The Context of the Early Cryptocurrency Landscape: To understand the genesis of Ixcoin, we provide a contextual overview of the cryptocurrency landscape during the early 2010s. We explore the influence of Bitcoin's emergence and the broader interest in decentralized digital currencies that paved the way for Ixcoin's creation.

1.2 Founding Vision and Objectives: We dive into the founding vision and objectives that set the stage for Ixcoin's development. We explore the motivations behind the creation of a global decentralized currency, including the desire to provide financial sovereignty, foster peer-to-peer transactions, and challenge the traditional financial system's centralized control.

2. Technical Foundations:

2.1 Blockchain Technology: Ixcoin, like many cryptocurrencies, was built on blockchain technology. We delve into the technical foundations of Ixcoin's blockchain, exploring its architecture, consensus mechanism, and key features. By understanding the technical aspects of Ixcoin, we gain insights into the underlying infrastructure that supports its decentralized nature.

2.2 Mining and Security: Mining plays a crucial role in the security and operation of Ixcoin's blockchain. We explore the mining process, the role of miners in validating transactions and maintaining the network, and the security implications of Ixcoin's Proof-of-Work consensus algorithm. Additionally, we examine any notable advancements or modifications in Ixcoin's mining process throughout its development.

3. Development Milestones:

3.1 Launch and Initial Distribution: We explore the launch of Ixcoin, including its initial distribution and the mechanisms used to ensure a fair and equitable distribution of coins. We delve into the factors that influenced the early adoption and growth of Ixcoin within the cryptocurrency community.

3.2 Technical Upgrades and Enhancements: The development of Ixcoin did not stop at its initial launch. We examine the major technical upgrades and enhancements that were implemented over time. This includes improvements to the blockchain protocol, the introduction of new features, and any notable upgrades that aimed to address scalability, security, or usability concerns.

4. Community and Governance:

4.1 Community Engagement and Collaboration: The Ixcoin community played an essential role in its development. We explore the dynamics of the Ixcoin community, including the involvement of developers, miners, users, and enthusiasts. We analyze community-driven initiatives, collaborations, and the role of open-source contributions in shaping the direction of Ixcoin.

4.2 Governance and Decision-Making: Ixcoin's governance model influenced its development and decision-making processes. We delve into the governance structures and mechanisms employed by Ixcoin, including community governance, consensus-building, and decision-making protocols. We explore how decisions were made and the community's involvement in shaping the trajectory of Ixcoin.

5. Impact and Legacy:

5.1 Influence on Decentralization: Ixcoin's development and adoption contributed to the broader movement towards decentralization in the cryptocurrency ecosystem. We evaluate its impact on decentralization, exploring how Ixcoin's existence and principles influenced the development of subsequent cryptocurrencies and decentralized finance initiatives.

5.2 Lessons Learned and Evolution: As Ixcoin evolved, it encountered challenges and underwent changes. We reflect on the lessons learned throughout its development, highlighting the adaptations made to address technological, regulatory, or market challenges. By examining its evolution, we gain insights into the resilience and adaptability of Ixcoin as a global decentralized currency.

Conclusion:

In this concluding section of Chapter 1, we reflect on the genesis and development of Ixcoin. We summarize the key insights gained from exploring its origins, technical foundations, development milestones, community dynamics, and impact. By understanding the story behind Ixcoin's creation and development, we gain a deeper appreciation for its role in shaping the cryptocurrency landscape and advancing the concept of global decentralized currencies.

Adoption and Community Engagement

In this chapter, we explore the adoption and community engagement surrounding Ixcoin, an early cryptocurrency that aimed to establish itself as a global decentralized currency. We delve into the factors that influenced its adoption, the dynamics of the Ixcoin community, and the initiatives that drove its growth. Join us as we uncover the story of Ixcoin's journey through adoption and community engagement.

1. Early Adoption and Growth:

1.1 Initial Reception: We examine the early adoption of Ixcoin within the cryptocurrency community. We explore the factors that initially attracted users, miners, and enthusiasts to Ixcoin, such as its unique features, principles, or technological advancements. Additionally, we assess the challenges faced during the early stages of adoption and how the community responded to overcome them.

1.2 Market Presence and Exchanges: Ixcoin's presence in the cryptocurrency market is a significant indicator of its adoption. We analyze the exchanges where Ixcoin was listed, exploring its trading volume, liquidity, and market capitalization during different phases of its existence. We also assess the impact of market factors, such as price volatility or regulatory developments, on Ixcoin's adoption trajectory.

2. Community Dynamics:

2.1 Developer Community: Developers play a vital role in the growth and evolution of cryptocurrencies. We explore the involvement of developers within the Ixcoin community, assessing their contributions to the project's codebase, technical improvements, and the overall development roadmap. We delve into the collaboration and communication channels established by the developer community to foster innovation and progress.

2.2 Mining Community: Mining is an integral part of Ixcoin's ecosystem. We delve into the mining community that supported Ixcoin, examining the mining pools, mining hardware used, and the incentives provided to miners. Additionally, we explore the role of mining in securing the network, maintaining consensus, and the influence of mining on Ixcoin's distribution and decentralization goals.

2.3 User Engagement and Adoption: The engagement of users is crucial for the success of any cryptocurrency. We analyze the user adoption and engagement within the Ixcoin community, exploring the user experience, wallets available, and user-friendly features that contributed to its adoption. We also examine user-driven initiatives, such as merchant adoption, community events, or educational resources, that helped to expand Ixcoin's user base.

3. Community-Driven Initiatives:

3.1 Community Governance and Decision-Making: Ixcoin's community played an active role in shaping its development and direction. We explore the governance mechanisms and decision-making processes employed by the Ixcoin community. This includes consensus-building, voting systems, and the participation of community members in proposing and implementing changes to the protocol.

3.2 Community Events and Initiatives: Community-driven events and initiatives fostered engagement and awareness around Ixcoin. We highlight notable community-led activities, such as meetups, conferences, hackathons, or online forums, that brought together Ixcoin enthusiasts, developers, and stakeholders. We also examine the impact of these initiatives on fostering collaboration, knowledge sharing, and the overall growth of the Ixcoin community.

4. Adoption in Real-World Use Cases:

4.1 Merchant Adoption: We explore the adoption of Ixcoin as a medium of exchange by merchants and businesses. We analyze the industries or sectors where Ixcoin found practical use, such as e-commerce, remittances, or peer-to-peer transactions. Additionally, we assess the challenges and opportunities encountered in promoting merchant adoption and the strategies employed by the Ixcoin community to overcome them.

4.2 Community Contributions and Philanthropy: Ixcoin's community was known for its philanthropic efforts and contributions. We delve into the charitable initiatives, donations, or community-driven projects supported by Ixcoin. We explore how the community leveraged the principles of decentralization and financial sovereignty to make a positive impact in various humanitarian or social causes.

5. Reflections on Community Engagement:

5.1 Lessons Learned and Best Practices: By examining the adoption and community engagement surrounding Ixcoin, we reflect on the lessons learned and best practices that emerged from its journey. We identify key strategies or approaches that contributed to successful community building, adoption, and sustained engagement.

5.2 Community Resilience and Evolution: The Ixcoin community faced numerous challenges and adaptations throughout its existence. We reflect on the resilience and evolution of the community, analyzing how it responded to external factors, internal dynamics, and market changes. By understanding the community's journey, we gain insights into the long-term sustainability and adaptability of decentralized cryptocurrencies.

Conclusion:

In this concluding section of Chapter 1, we reflect on the adoption and community engagement surrounding Ixcoin. We summarize the key insights gained from exploring its early adoption, community dynamics, community-driven initiatives, real-world use cases, and the lessons learned from community engagement. By understanding the role of the community in Ixcoin's development, we gain a deeper appreciation for the decentralized nature and community-driven ethos of this global decentralized currency.

Evaluating Ixcoin's Role in the Cryptocurrency Ecosystem

In this chapter, we evaluate the role of Ixcoin in the broader cryptocurrency ecosystem. We assess its impact, contributions, and challenges in shaping the development of decentralized digital currencies. Join us as we delve into the evaluation of Ixcoin's significance and its position in the evolving landscape of cryptocurrencies.

1. Unique Features and Contributions:

1.1 Differentiating Factors: Ixcoin aimed to establish itself as a global decentralized currency, distinguishing itself from other cryptocurrencies through its unique features. We explore the specific attributes that set Ixcoin apart from its counterparts, such as transaction speed, scalability, privacy features, or governance model. We evaluate the significance of these features and their impact on Ixcoin's role in the cryptocurrency ecosystem.

1.2 Advancements in Technology: Ixcoin's development may have introduced technological advancements or innovations to the cryptocurrency space. We examine any notable technical contributions made by Ixcoin, including improvements to the underlying blockchain technology, consensus mechanisms, or scalability solutions.

We assess the implications of these advancements and their influence on the wider cryptocurrency ecosystem.

2. Interactions with Other Cryptocurrencies:

2.1 Synergies and Collaborations: Cryptocurrencies often interact and collaborate with one another to foster innovation and growth. We explore the collaborations, partnerships, or interoperability efforts involving Ixcoin and other cryptocurrencies. We examine the synergies created through these interactions and how they contributed to the overall development and adoption of decentralized digital currencies.

2.2 Competitive Landscape: The cryptocurrency ecosystem is highly competitive, with numerous cryptocurrencies vying for market share and attention. We evaluate Ixcoin's position in the competitive landscape, analyzing its strengths, weaknesses, opportunities, and threats in relation to other cryptocurrencies. We examine the factors that influenced its competitiveness and its ability to differentiate itself from other projects.

3. Market Perception and Adoption:

3.1 Market Perception: The perception of Ixcoin within the cryptocurrency market plays a significant role in its adoption and long-term viability. We assess the market's perception of Ixcoin, including investor sentiment, media coverage, and community sentiment. We explore the factors that influenced the perception of Ixcoin and how it impacted its adoption and market positioning.

3.2 Adoption and User Base: The adoption of Ixcoin by users is a crucial factor in evaluating its role in the cryptocurrency ecosystem. We examine the growth of Ixcoin's user base, analyzing factors that contributed to its adoption, such as ease of use, utility, or community engagement. We also explore the geographic distribution of Ixcoin's adoption and its significance in different regions.

4. Challenges and Lessons Learned:

4.1 Technical Challenges and Solutions: Like any cryptocurrency, Ixcoin faced technical challenges during its development and adoption. We identify and evaluate the technical challenges encountered by Ixcoin, such as scalability limitations, security vulnerabilities, or network congestion. We assess the solutions implemented to address these challenges and the lessons learned from navigating them.

4.2 Regulatory and Legal Considerations: Regulatory and legal factors can significantly impact the role of a cryptocurrency in the wider ecosystem. We examine the regulatory challenges faced by Ixcoin, such as compliance with financial regulations or government scrutiny. We explore how Ixcoin addressed these challenges and the implications for its role in the cryptocurrency ecosystem.

5. Future Prospects and Outlook:

5.1 Evolutionary Potential: We assess the evolutionary potential of Ixcoin, considering its current state and future development roadmap. We analyze the potential for further technological advancements, scalability solutions, or collaborations that could enhance Ixcoin's role in the cryptocurrency ecosystem.

5.2 Impact on the Digital Economy: Finally, we evaluate Ixcoin's impact on the digital economy. We explore its potential to disrupt traditional financial systems, empower individuals with financial sovereignty, or enable new forms of economic interactions. We reflect on the broader implications of Ixcoin's role in shaping the digital economy and its potential to foster financial inclusion and innovation.

Conclusion:

In this concluding section of Chapter 1, we reflect on the evaluation of Ixcoin's role in the cryptocurrency ecosystem. We summarize the key insights gained from exploring its unique features, interactions with other cryptocurrencies, market perception, adoption, challenges faced, and future prospects. By understanding Ixcoin's position in the broader ecosystem, we gain a deeper appreciation for its contributions and significance as a global decentralized currency.

Chapter 2: Freicoin (FRC), established 2012 - "Demurrage currency with distribution mechanisms."

Understanding Freicoin's Demurrage Currency with Distribution Mechanisms

In this chapter, we delve into the unique characteristics of Freicoin, a cryptocurrency established in 2012 with a demurrage currency model and innovative distribution mechanisms. We explore the concept of demurrage and its purpose within the Freicoin ecosystem. Join us as we unravel the intricacies of Freicoin's demurrage currency system and its impact on economic dynamics and distribution mechanisms.

1. Demurrage Currency and its Significance:

1.1 Demurrage as a Concept: We begin by providing an overview of demurrage currency and its underlying principles. We explain how demurrage aims to encourage circulation and prevent hoarding by introducing a regular depreciation of the currency over time. We explore the historical context of demurrage currency and its relevance to modern economic systems.

1.2 Freicoin's Demurrage Currency Model: Freicoin implemented a demurrage currency model as its core economic mechanism. We examine the specific implementation of demurrage within Freicoin, including the rate of depreciation, calculation methods, and its impact on the value and circulation of the currency. We assess the motivations behind choosing demurrage as the foundational principle for Freicoin.

2. Economic Implications and Dynamics:

2.1 Encouraging Circulation and Velocity of Money: The demurrage currency model employed by Freicoin aims to stimulate the velocity of money, facilitating economic transactions and discouraging hoarding. We explore how the demurrage mechanism influences the behavior of users, businesses, and investors in the Freicoin ecosystem. We analyze the impact on the velocity of money, the frequency of transactions, and the potential benefits for economic growth.

2.2 Inflation and Deflation Perspectives: Demurrage currency models can have contrasting effects on inflation and deflation. We evaluate the inflationary and deflationary aspects of Freicoin's demurrage mechanism, examining the implications for price stability, monetary policy, and macroeconomic dynamics. We also assess the challenges and opportunities associated with managing inflationary pressures within the Freicoin ecosystem.

3. Distribution Mechanisms:

3.1 Initial Distribution: We explore the distribution mechanisms employed during the launch of Freicoin. We examine the methods used to distribute the initial supply of coins, such as airdrops, mining rewards, or community allocations. We analyze the rationale behind the chosen distribution mechanisms and their impact on the initial adoption and community engagement.

3.2 Redistribution and Economic Justice: Freicoin introduced innovative distribution mechanisms to promote economic justice and equitable wealth distribution. We delve into the mechanisms implemented to redistribute the currency over time, including mechanisms like universal basic income or community grants. We evaluate the effectiveness of these redistribution mechanisms and their impact on social and economic equality within the Freicoin ecosystem.

4. Use Cases and Adoption:

4.1 Real-World Applications: We examine the use cases and adoption of Freicoin in practical applications. We explore industries, sectors, or communities that embraced Freicoin's demurrage currency model and the reasons behind their adoption. We analyze the benefits and challenges encountered when integrating Freicoin into real-world economic systems.

4.2 Challenges and Future Prospects: We assess the challenges faced by Freicoin in its journey towards adoption and mainstream recognition. We examine the barriers encountered, such as regulatory hurdles, market perception, or scalability limitations. Additionally, we explore the future prospects of Freicoin, including potential areas of growth, partnerships, or technological advancements that could drive its adoption and expand its impact.

5. Reflections on Freicoin's Demurrage Model:

In this section, we reflect on the unique aspects of Freicoin's demurrage currency model. We summarize the key insights gained from understanding the purpose of demurrage, its economic implications, and the innovative distribution mechanisms implemented by Freicoin. By comprehending the intricacies of Freicoin's demurrage system, we gain a deeper understanding of its potential to shape economic dynamics and foster equitable distribution within the cryptocurrency ecosystem.

Conclusion:

In this concluding section of Chapter 2, we reflect on the significance of Freicoin's demurrage currency model and distribution mechanisms. We summarize the key takeaways from exploring the concept of demurrage, the economic implications, and the unique distribution mechanisms employed by Freicoin. By understanding the intricacies of Freicoin's demurrage system, we gain insights into its potential contributions to the broader cryptocurrency landscape and its role in shaping economic systems based on equitable distribution and incentivized circulation.

Exploring the Concept of Demurrage and Its Purpose

In this chapter, we delve into the concept of demurrage and its purpose within the Freicoin ecosystem. We explore the origins of demurrage currency, its historical context, and its relevance in the modern economic landscape. Join us as we unravel the intricacies of demurrage and its significance in fostering circulation, economic dynamics, and equitable distribution.

1. Understanding Demurrage Currency:

1.1 Historical Context: We begin by providing a historical overview of demurrage currency. We explore its origins and its application in different periods of history. We examine notable examples of demurrage currency in practice and the motivations behind their implementation. Understanding the historical context of demurrage currency provides valuable insights into its purpose and potential advantages.

1.2 Demurrage Explained: We delve into the concept of demurrage itself, explaining its core principles and mechanics. We examine how demurrage aims to encourage circulation and discourage hoarding of currency. We explore the fundamental aspects of demurrage, such as the rate of depreciation, calculation methods, and the impact on the value of the currency over time. By understanding the mechanics of demurrage, we gain a deeper appreciation for its purpose and implications.

2. Economic Rationale for Demurrage:

2.1 Encouraging Circulation: One of the primary purposes of demurrage currency is to stimulate circulation. We examine how demurrage achieves this goal by incentivizing individuals to spend or invest their currency rather than hoarding it. We analyze the economic rationale behind encouraging circulation and the potential benefits it brings to economic dynamics, such as increased liquidity and economic activity.

2.2 Promoting Currency Velocity: Demurrage currency models aim to promote the velocity of money, facilitating economic transactions and enhancing overall economic health. We explore how demurrage incentivizes the rapid turnover of currency by discouraging long-term holding. We examine the impact of increased currency velocity on economic growth, investment, and entrepreneurial activities.

3. Stability and Inflation Considerations:

3.1 Price Stability: Demurrage currency models may have implications for price stability. We examine how the regular depreciation of currency affects the stability of prices within an economy. We analyze the potential advantages and challenges of maintaining price stability within a demurrage system and the role of monetary policy in managing inflationary pressures.

3.2 Addressing Inflation and Deflation: Demurrage currency can provide unique solutions to address inflation and deflation. We explore how demurrage mechanisms mitigate the risk of excessive inflation or deflationary pressures. We assess the benefits of a demurrage system in managing monetary supply and the challenges associated with maintaining a balanced economic environment.

4. Societal Implications:

4.1 Encouraging Social Equity: Demurrage currency models often aim to promote social equity by redistributing wealth and resources more equitably. We examine how demurrage facilitates a more equal distribution of currency over time, potentially reducing wealth disparities. We analyze the potential impact of demurrage on socioeconomic dynamics and the challenges and opportunities associated with implementing equitable distribution mechanisms.

4.2 Economic and Environmental Sustainability: Demurrage currency models also have implications for economic and environmental sustainability. We explore how demurrage can incentivize sustainable economic practices, such as investment in productive activities and discouragement of speculative behaviors. We also examine how demurrage currency aligns with concepts of resource conservation and environmental stewardship.

5. Criticisms and Controversies:

5.1 Critiques of Demurrage Currency: We present an analysis of the criticisms and controversies surrounding demurrage currency models. We explore common concerns, such as potential negative effects on saving behavior, challenges in implementing and managing demurrage, and the implications for financial stability. We critically assess these arguments and provide a balanced perspective on the limitations and trade-offs associated with demurrage currency.

Conclusion:

In this concluding section of Chapter 2, we reflect on the exploration of the concept of demurrage and its purpose within the Freicoin ecosystem. We summarize the key insights gained from understanding the historical context, economic rationale, stability considerations, societal implications, and critiques of demurrage currency. By comprehending the intricacies of demurrage, we gain a deeper understanding of its purpose in fostering circulation, equitable distribution, and sustainable economic dynamics within the Freicoin ecosystem and beyond.

Use Cases and Adoption in Economic Systems

In this section, we explore the various use cases and adoption of Freicoin (FRC) within economic systems. We examine the practical applications of demurrage currency and the impact it has on different sectors of the economy. By analyzing real-world examples and case studies, we gain insights into the potential benefits and challenges of implementing Freicoin in economic systems.

1. Local and Community Economies:

1.1 Local Currencies: We explore how Freicoin can be utilized as a local currency within community economies. We examine the role of local currencies in supporting regional businesses, promoting local trade, and fostering community resilience. We analyze the advantages of using demurrage currency in localized economic systems and the potential for increased circulation and economic activity.

1.2 Complementary Currencies: We discuss how Freicoin can function as a complementary currency alongside national fiat currencies. We explore the benefits of introducing demurrage currency as a means to stimulate economic transactions, encourage local production, and strengthen local economies. We analyze case studies of successful complementary currency systems that have incorporated demurrage principles.

2. Social and Environmental Initiatives:

2.1 Sustainable Development: We examine how Freicoin can be utilized to support sustainable development initiatives. We explore the potential for demurrage currency to incentivize investments in environmentally friendly projects, renewable energy, and sustainable agriculture. We analyze examples of organizations and communities that have successfully integrated demurrage currency in their sustainability efforts.

2.2 Social Impact: We discuss the social impact of Freicoin and its potential to address social issues. We examine how demurrage currency can be used to fund social programs, support community projects, and address income inequality. We explore case studies of initiatives that have leveraged demurrage currency to promote social justice and empowerment.

3. Economic Systems and Policy Considerations:

3.1 Macroeconomic Implications: We analyze the macroeconomic implications of integrating Freicoin into economic systems. We examine how demurrage currency can affect monetary policy, inflation, and economic stability. We explore the challenges and opportunities associated with incorporating demurrage into existing economic frameworks and discuss potential policy considerations.

3.2 Financial Inclusion: We discuss the potential for Freicoin to promote financial inclusion, particularly in underserved communities. We explore how demurrage currency can provide access to financial services for individuals who are unbanked or underbanked. We analyze case studies of projects that have successfully used demurrage currency to foster financial inclusion.

4. International Trade and Cooperation:

4.1 Cross-Border Transactions: We examine the potential for Freicoin to facilitate cross-border transactions and international trade. We discuss how demurrage currency can mitigate currency fluctuations, reduce transaction costs, and promote trade between countries. We explore case studies of initiatives that have leveraged demurrage currency in international trade settings.

4.2 Collaboration and Partnerships: We analyze the possibilities for collaboration and partnerships between Freicoin and other organizations, governments, or cryptocurrencies. We discuss potential synergies and cooperative efforts to advance demurrage currency adoption and explore opportunities for cross-pollination of ideas and initiatives.

Conclusion:

In this concluding section of Chapter 2, we reflect on the various use cases and adoption of Freicoin within economic systems. We summarize the key insights gained from exploring the practical applications of demurrage currency in local and community economies, social and environmental initiatives, economic systems, and international trade. By comprehending the diverse use cases and adoption of Freicoin, we gain a deeper understanding of its potential contributions to fostering economic resilience, sustainability, financial inclusion, and global cooperation.

Challenges and Future Prospects of Freicoin

In this section, we explore the challenges and future prospects of Freicoin (FRC) as a demurrage currency with distribution mechanisms. We examine the obstacles and hurdles that Freicoin has faced throughout its existence and discuss potential strategies for addressing these challenges. Additionally, we delve into the future outlook of Freicoin, considering its potential for growth, scalability, and broader adoption.

1. Technical Challenges:

1.1 Scalability: We examine the scalability challenges that Freicoin faces as its user base and transaction volume grow. We discuss the limitations of the current infrastructure and explore potential solutions for enhancing the scalability of the Freicoin network. We analyze technological advancements, such as layer-2 solutions or protocol upgrades, that could enable Freicoin to handle a larger number of transactions efficiently.

1.2 Network Security: We discuss the importance of network security in the context of Freicoin and the challenges associated with maintaining a robust and secure network. We examine potential vulnerabilities and attack vectors that could threaten the integrity of the network. We explore strategies for strengthening network security, such as consensus algorithm enhancements or the integration of advanced cryptographic techniques.

2. Regulatory and Legal Considerations:

2.1 Regulatory Landscape: We explore the evolving regulatory landscape surrounding cryptocurrencies and the potential challenges and compliance requirements faced by Freicoin. We discuss the impact of regulatory measures, such as anti-money laundering (AML) and know-your-customer (KYC) regulations, on the adoption and use of Freicoin. We analyze how Freicoin can navigate regulatory challenges while remaining true to its principles of decentralization and privacy.

2.2 Legal Status and Recognition: We discuss the legal status and recognition of Freicoin in various jurisdictions. We examine the challenges of achieving legal recognition and how it can impact the adoption and acceptance of Freicoin in traditional economic systems. We explore potential strategies for engaging with regulatory bodies and policymakers to foster a favorable legal environment for Freicoin.

3. Adoption and Market Challenges:

3.1 User Adoption: We discuss the challenges of driving user adoption of Freicoin and expanding its user base. We analyze the factors that influence user adoption, such as user experience, education, and awareness. We explore strategies for promoting Freicoin and increasing its appeal to a broader audience, including marketing initiatives, partnerships, and user-friendly wallets and applications.

3.2 Market Volatility: We examine the issue of market volatility and its impact on Freicoin. We discuss the challenges of maintaining stability in the value of demurrage currency, considering the fluctuations and speculation commonly associated with cryptocurrencies. We explore potential mechanisms for mitigating market volatility and ensuring a more stable value for Freicoin.

4. Community and Governance:

4.1 Community Engagement: We discuss the importance of community engagement in the success and growth of Freicoin. We explore the challenges of maintaining an active and supportive community and fostering participation and collaboration. We analyze strategies for enhancing community engagement, such as incentivization mechanisms, community initiatives, and transparent governance structures.

4.2 Governance Mechanisms: We examine the governance mechanisms of Freicoin and the challenges associated with decentralized decision-making. We discuss the balance between decentralization and efficient governance, exploring potential improvements to the governance structure of Freicoin. We analyze different models, such as on-chain governance or delegated voting, that could enhance community participation and decision-making processes.

5. Future Prospects:

5.1 Innovation and Development: We discuss the potential for innovation and development within the Freicoin ecosystem. We explore areas for improvement, such as user experience, scalability, privacy features, and integration with emerging technologies like blockchain interoperability or smart contracts. We analyze potential avenues for collaboration and technological advancements that could enhance the future prospects of Freicoin.

5.2 Broader Adoption and Impact: We discuss the future potential for broader adoption of Freicoin beyond niche communities. We explore the opportunities for Freicoin to make a significant impact in traditional financial systems, global trade, and economic empowerment. We analyze the potential benefits of demurrage currency in addressing societal challenges and fostering sustainable economic dynamics.

Conclusion:

In this concluding section of Chapter 2, we reflect on the challenges and future prospects of Freicoin as a demurrage currency with distribution mechanisms. We summarize the key insights gained from discussing the technical, regulatory, adoption, market, community, and governance challenges faced by Freicoin. Additionally, we explore the potential for future growth, innovation, and broader adoption of Freicoin in the ever-evolving cryptocurrency and economic landscape.

Chapter 3: Dogecoin (DOGE), established 2013 - "The fun and friendly internet currency."

From Meme to Mainstream: The Journey of Dogecoin

In this section, we delve into the captivating journey of Dogecoin (DOGE) from its humble origins as a meme to its rise as a mainstream cryptocurrency. We explore the factors that contributed to Dogecoin's popularity and examine how it evolved from a lighthearted community project to a significant player in the crypto industry. We also discuss the impact of Dogecoin's unique branding and community-driven initiatives on its success.

1. The Birth of Dogecoin:

1.1 The Origin Story: We explore the background and creation of Dogecoin, tracing its roots back to the popular "Doge" meme and the collaborative efforts of Billy Markus and Jackson Palmer. We discuss the motivations behind the creation of Dogecoin and the initial vision for the project.

1.2 The Role of Community: We highlight the pivotal role played by the Dogecoin community in the early days of the cryptocurrency. We examine how the welcoming and inclusive nature of the community attracted a broad range of users and fostered a sense of camaraderie and shared enthusiasm.

2. The Rise of Dogecoin:

2.1 Viral Awareness and Tipping Culture: We discuss the viral nature of Dogecoin and how it gained widespread attention through social media platforms and online communities. We explore the concept of "tipping" and the unique tipping culture that emerged around Dogecoin, where users would tip each other with small amounts of DOGE as a gesture of appreciation or support.

2.2 Fundraising and Philanthropy: We delve into Dogecoin's reputation for charitable giving and fundraising initiatives. We examine notable examples, such as the Dogecoin community raising funds for the Jamaican bobsled team and supporting various charitable causes. We analyze the impact of these initiatives on Dogecoin's visibility and public perception.

3. Dogecoin's Market Performance:

3.1 Market Volatility and Speculation: We discuss the market dynamics surrounding Dogecoin, including its notable price fluctuations and the speculative nature of its trading activity. We analyze the factors that have contributed to Dogecoin's price volatility and its perception as a high-risk investment.

3.2 Influences from External Factors: We explore the influence of external factors on Dogecoin's market performance. This includes the impact of celebrity endorsements, social media trends, and broader market conditions. We analyze the effects of these influences on Dogecoin's price movements and investor sentiment.

4. Dogecoin's Cultural Impact:

4.1 Internet Culture and Memes: We examine how Dogecoin's association with internet culture and memes has shaped its identity and appeal. We discuss the role of memes in fostering a sense of community and creating a relatable and accessible image for Dogecoin.

4.2 Dogecoin in Pop Culture: We explore Dogecoin's appearances in mainstream media and popular culture. We discuss instances where Dogecoin was mentioned or referenced in television shows, movies, and music, and examine the impact of these cultural references on Dogecoin's recognition and adoption.

5. Dogecoin's Future Potential:

5.1 Technological Advancements and Development: We discuss the ongoing development of Dogecoin's technology and the potential for implementing new features or improvements. We analyze the challenges and opportunities associated with enhancing Dogecoin's scalability, security, and functionality to meet the demands of a growing user base.

5.2 Broader Adoption and Integration: We explore the potential for Dogecoin to achieve broader adoption beyond its existing user base. We discuss partnerships, collaborations, and integrations that could facilitate the use of Dogecoin in everyday transactions and enhance its utility as a digital currency.

Conclusion:

In this concluding section of Chapter 3, we reflect on the journey of Dogecoin from a meme to a mainstream cryptocurrency. We summarize the key milestones and factors that have contributed to Dogecoin's success, including its vibrant community, viral awareness, philanthropic initiatives, and cultural impact. Additionally, we speculate on Dogecoin's future potential and its role in shaping the digital economy.

The Fun and Friendly Internet Currency

In this section, we delve into the unique characteristics that have earned Dogecoin (DOGE) the reputation of being the "fun and friendly internet currency." We explore the origins of Dogecoin's lighthearted nature, its community-driven initiatives, and the impact of its friendly branding. We also examine how these attributes have contributed to Dogecoin's popularity and widespread adoption.

1. The Lighter Side of Dogecoin:

1.1 A Playful and Approachable Brand: We discuss the distinct branding of Dogecoin that sets it apart from other cryptocurrencies. We analyze the elements of the Dogecoin logo, the iconic Shiba Inu dog, and the use of comic sans font, all of which contribute to the playful and approachable image of Dogecoin.

1.2 Memes and Internet Culture: We explore the connection between Dogecoin and internet culture, particularly memes. We discuss how the Dogecoin community embraced memes and incorporated them into the narrative surrounding the cryptocurrency. We analyze the role of memes in creating a sense of camaraderie, humor, and relatability within the Dogecoin community.

2. Community-Driven Initiatives:

2.1 Tipping Culture: We delve into the tipping culture that emerged within the Dogecoin community. We discuss how Dogecoin's low transaction fees and abundance of coins made it ideal for microtransactions and tipping. We explore the social aspect of tipping and the positive impact it had on fostering engagement and spreading awareness about Dogecoin.

2.2 Philanthropy and Fundraising: We highlight Dogecoin's reputation for philanthropic initiatives and fundraising efforts. We discuss notable examples, such as the Dogecoin community's support for charitable causes and disaster relief efforts. We analyze how these initiatives not only showcased the generosity of the Dogecoin community but also increased the visibility and credibility of the cryptocurrency.

3. The Power of the Dogecoin Community:

3.1 Inclusivity and Support: We examine the inclusive and supportive nature of the Dogecoin community. We discuss how the community welcomed newcomers, provided educational resources, and encouraged participation. We explore the role of online forums, social media platforms, and dedicated Dogecoin communities in facilitating communication and collaboration.

3.2 Community Projects and Initiatives: We highlight the various community projects and initiatives that have emerged within the Dogecoin ecosystem. We discuss initiatives such as Dogecoin-sponsored NASCAR races, community-funded development projects, and collaborations with other organizations. We analyze the positive impact of these initiatives on Dogecoin's branding, adoption, and community cohesion.

4. Dogecoin's Cultural Impact:

4.1 Memeification of Finance: We explore how Dogecoin's association with memes and internet culture has contributed to the memeification of finance. We discuss the broader cultural implications of the blending of traditional finance and online communities, and the role Dogecoin has played in challenging the perception of cryptocurrency as a serious and exclusive domain.

4.2 Popularity Among Online Communities: We examine the popularity of Dogecoin within various online communities. We discuss how Dogecoin has gained traction among social media platforms, gaming communities, and forums. We analyze the impact of this popularity on Dogecoin's user base, market value, and overall awareness.

5. Dogecoin's Enduring Appeal:

5.1 Mainstream Recognition and Acceptance: We explore the increasing recognition and acceptance of Dogecoin by mainstream entities. We discuss partnerships with companies, brands, and charitable organizations that have embraced Dogecoin as a means of payment or donation. We analyze how these partnerships have contributed to Dogecoin's legitimacy and long-term viability.

5.2 Dogecoin's Role in Financial Education: We discuss how Dogecoin's user-friendly nature and community-driven initiatives have played a role in promoting financial education and literacy. We examine how Dogecoin has introduced newcomers to the world of cryptocurrencies, blockchain technology, and decentralized finance.

Conclusion:

In this concluding section of Chapter 3, we reflect on the journey of Dogecoin as the "fun and friendly internet currency." We summarize the key characteristics that have contributed to Dogecoin's unique appeal, including its lighthearted branding, community-driven initiatives, and cultural impact. We also discuss the challenges and opportunities that lie ahead for Dogecoin as it continues to evolve and carve out its niche in the digital economy.

Community-driven Initiatives and Philanthropy

In this section, we explore the remarkable community-driven initiatives and philanthropic endeavors that have become synonymous with Dogecoin (DOGE). We delve into the history of Dogecoin's community, their passion for making a positive impact, and the numerous projects and charitable initiatives they have undertaken. We examine how the Dogecoin community's collective efforts have propelled the cryptocurrency to new heights and distinguished it within the broader crypto landscape.

1. The Spirit of Giving:

1.1 Generosity at the Core: We delve into the origins of Dogecoin's philanthropic nature and examine how the community's spirit of giving has been a fundamental aspect from the early days. We discuss the ethos of generosity and compassion that permeates the Dogecoin community and sets it apart from other cryptocurrencies.

1.2 The Power of Microdonations: We explore the concept of microdonations and how Dogecoin's low transaction fees and large coin supply have enabled the community to engage in widespread giving. We examine how the ability to send small amounts of Dogecoin has facilitated charitable acts on various scales, from individual projects to larger fundraising initiatives.

2. Notable Philanthropic Endeavors:

2.1 Dogecoin's Early Philanthropy: We delve into the early philanthropic endeavors of the Dogecoin community and highlight significant projects that helped establish Dogecoin's reputation for giving. We discuss notable initiatives such as the Dogecoin Foundation, which supported causes such as clean water, education, and disaster relief efforts.

2.2 Dogecoin's Impact on Individual Lives: We share stories of individuals whose lives have been positively impacted by the Dogecoin community's philanthropy. We highlight instances where the community rallied together to provide financial assistance for medical treatments, educational scholarships, and other life-changing endeavors.

3. Community-driven Projects:

3.1 The Dogecoin Community's Collaborative Spirit: We explore the collaborative nature of the Dogecoin community and how it has given rise to various community-driven projects. We discuss initiatives such as Dogecoin-sponsored sports teams, art projects, online games, and crowdfunding campaigns that have fostered engagement and creativity within the community.

3.2 The Dogecoin Socks for the Homeless Initiative: We highlight the Dogecoin community's notable Socks for the Homeless initiative as a case study. We examine how this grassroots project gained traction and garnered significant support from the Dogecoin community, resulting in the distribution of socks and other essential items to homeless individuals.

4. Partnerships with Charitable Organizations:

4.1 Collaborations with Established Charities: We discuss the partnerships between the Dogecoin community and established charitable organizations. We explore how these collaborations have expanded the reach and impact of Dogecoin's philanthropic efforts. We examine examples of partnerships with organizations such as Save the Children, Charity: Water, and the Binance Charity Foundation.

4.2 Fundraising Campaigns and Donations: We examine the various fundraising campaigns and donation drives initiated by the Dogecoin community. We discuss instances where the community rallied together to raise funds for disaster relief, humanitarian causes, animal welfare, and other charitable endeavors.

5. Impact and Recognition:

5.1 Social Impact and Awareness: We analyze the social impact generated by the Dogecoin community's philanthropic initiatives. We examine how the community's generosity and commitment to making a difference have garnered media attention and increased awareness of Dogecoin among a wider audience.

5.2 Recognition from Charitable Organizations: We highlight instances where the Dogecoin community's philanthropic efforts have been recognized by charitable organizations. We discuss how these organizations have embraced Dogecoin as a legitimate and impactful force for positive change.

Conclusion:

In this concluding section of Chapter 3, we reflect on the profound impact of Dogecoin's community-driven initiatives and philanthropy. We emphasize how the Dogecoin community's passion for giving has not only shaped the image of Dogecoin but has also demonstrated the potential for cryptocurrencies to be a force for good in the world. We discuss the lasting legacy of Dogecoin's philanthropic endeavors and the potential for future projects to continue making a positive impact on individuals and communities worldwide.

Dogecoin's Cultural Impact and Future Potential

In this section, we explore the cultural impact of Dogecoin (DOGE) and its potential for the future. We examine how Dogecoin's unique characteristics and community-driven nature have contributed to its widespread recognition and adoption. We also discuss the challenges and opportunities that lie ahead for Dogecoin as it continues to evolve in the ever-changing landscape of cryptocurrencies.

1. Dogecoin and Internet Culture:

1.1 The Birth of a Meme Coin: We delve into the origins of Dogecoin as a meme-based cryptocurrency and its connection to the popular "Doge" meme featuring the Shiba Inu dog. We discuss how this lighthearted and humorous branding resonated with internet culture and contributed to Dogecoin's initial popularity.

1.2 The Power of Virality: We explore how Dogecoin's meme-based nature and viral online presence played a significant role in its cultural impact. We discuss how social media platforms, online communities, and influencers helped propel Dogecoin into the mainstream consciousness.

2. The Dogecoin Community:

2.1 The Strength of a United Community: We examine the vibrant and dedicated community that has formed around Dogecoin. We discuss the inclusive and welcoming nature of the Dogecoin community, which has fostered a sense of belonging and camaraderie among its members.

2.2 Memes, Humor, and Engagement: We explore how memes, humor, and engaging content have been integral to the Dogecoin community's identity and its ability to capture the attention of a wide audience. We discuss the role of memes and humorous content in creating a sense of community and attracting new users to Dogecoin.

3. Dogecoin's Cultural References:

3.1 Dogecoin in Popular Media: We examine instances where Dogecoin has been referenced or featured in popular media, including television shows, movies, and music. We discuss how these cultural references have further solidified Dogecoin's presence in mainstream culture.

3.2 Dogecoin and Charitable Endeavors: We highlight the impact of Dogecoin's philanthropic initiatives on its cultural perception. We discuss how the community's charitable endeavors have contributed to the image of Dogecoin as a positive and socially responsible cryptocurrency.

4. Dogecoin's Integration and Adoption:

4.1 Merchant Acceptance and Use Cases: We explore the growing acceptance of Dogecoin by merchants and its integration into various industries. We discuss the use cases of Dogecoin as a means of payment, including online purchases, tipping content creators, and charitable donations.

4.2 Dogecoin's Influence on Other Cryptocurrencies: We examine how Dogecoin's cultural impact has influenced the development and adoption of other cryptocurrencies. We discuss the emergence of meme-based and community-driven coins inspired by Dogecoin's success.

5. Future Potential and Challenges:

5.1 Navigating Market Volatility: We discuss the challenges faced by Dogecoin in navigating the volatile cryptocurrency market. We examine how Dogecoin's community resilience and cultural impact have helped it withstand market fluctuations.

5.2 Long-Term Viability and Innovation: We analyze the future potential of Dogecoin and its ability to innovate and adapt to changing market trends. We discuss the challenges and opportunities for Dogecoin to remain relevant and sustainable in the long term.

Conclusion:

In this concluding section of Chapter 3, we reflect on the cultural impact of Dogecoin as the "fun and friendly internet currency." We summarize the key factors that have contributed to Dogecoin's cultural significance, including its meme-based origins, community engagement, and philanthropic endeavors. We also speculate on the future potential of Dogecoin, considering its evolving role in the cryptocurrency ecosystem and its ability to maintain its cultural relevance.

Chapter 4: Vertcoin (VTC), established 2014 - "Peer-to-peer digital currency with ASIC resistance."

Peer-to-Peer Digital Currency with ASIC Resistance

In this section, we explore Vertcoin (VTC), a peer-to-peer digital currency that has gained attention for its unique feature of ASIC resistance. We delve into the concept of ASIC resistance and its significance in promoting decentralization and fair mining practices. We discuss how Vertcoin's commitment to ASIC resistance sets it apart from other cryptocurrencies and examine the benefits it offers to the broader crypto ecosystem.

1. Understanding ASIC Resistance:

1.1 What are ASICs? We provide an overview of Application-Specific Integrated Circuits (ASICs) and their role in cryptocurrency mining. We discuss how ASICs have revolutionized mining by offering significant computational power, but also highlight their potential drawbacks in terms of centralization and mining efficiency.

1.2 The Need for ASIC Resistance: We explore the rationale behind the development of ASIC-resistant cryptocurrencies, including the concerns related to centralization of mining power and the exclusion of smaller miners. We discuss the importance of promoting a level playing field and decentralization in the crypto ecosystem.

2. Vertcoin's Approach to ASIC Resistance:

2.1 Vertcoin's Core Principles: We delve into the core principles that drive Vertcoin's development, focusing on its commitment to decentralization, fairness, and community involvement. We highlight how ASIC resistance aligns with these principles and contributes to the overall mission of Vertcoin.

2.2 Technical Implementation of ASIC Resistance: We discuss the technical measures employed by Vertcoin to achieve ASIC resistance. This includes the use of memory-intensive mining algorithms and periodic algorithm changes to deter ASIC manufacturers from gaining a significant advantage.

3. Benefits of ASIC Resistance:

3.1 Decentralization and Network Security: We explore how ASIC resistance promotes decentralization by allowing a broader range of individuals to participate in mining and securing the network. We discuss the benefits of a decentralized network in terms of security, resilience, and censorship resistance.

3.2 Empowering Individual Miners: We examine how ASIC resistance empowers individual miners by reducing the entry barrier and allowing them to mine using consumer-grade hardware. We discuss the potential for broader participation and engagement in the mining process.

4. ASIC Resistance and Fairness:

4.1 Mitigating Mining Centralization: We analyze how ASIC resistance mitigates the risk of mining centralization by preventing the concentration of mining power in the hands of a few entities. We discuss the potential consequences of mining centralization and how Vertcoin's ASIC resistance addresses these concerns.

4.2 Promoting Long-Term Network Stability: We discuss how ASIC resistance contributes to long-term network stability by preventing the rapid obsolescence of mining equipment. We explore the challenges associated with rapidly evolving ASIC technology and the benefits of a more sustainable mining ecosystem.

5. Adoption and Use Cases:

5.1 Vertcoin's Adoption in the Crypto Landscape: We examine the adoption of Vertcoin in the broader crypto landscape, including its listing on exchanges, wallet support, and community-driven initiatives. We discuss the challenges and opportunities Vertcoin faces in gaining wider recognition and integration.

5.2 Use Cases and Applications: We explore the various use cases and applications of Vertcoin beyond being a peer-to-peer digital currency. This includes potential applications in decentralized finance (DeFi), micropayments, and privacy-focused transactions.

Conclusion:

In this concluding section of Chapter 4, we summarize the key aspects of Vertcoin as a peer-to-peer digital currency with ASIC resistance. We highlight the significance of ASIC resistance in promoting decentralization, fair mining practices, and network security. We emphasize the potential impact of Vertcoin's approach on the broader crypto ecosystem and its role in fostering a more inclusive and resilient mining community.

The Need for ASIC Resistance and Decentralization

In this section, we delve into the significance of ASIC resistance and its relationship with the core principles of decentralization in the context of Vertcoin (VTC). We explore the challenges associated with ASIC mining and the potential risks of centralization. We discuss how Vertcoin's approach to ASIC resistance addresses these concerns and fosters a more decentralized and inclusive mining ecosystem.

1. Understanding ASIC Mining and Centralization:

1.1 What are ASICs and Their Advantages: We provide an overview of Application-Specific Integrated Circuits (ASICs) and their advantages in cryptocurrency mining, including their specialized hardware designed for specific mining algorithms. We discuss how ASICs have led to significant concentration of mining power in the hands of a few entities.

1.2 Risks of Centralization: We explore the risks associated with mining centralization, such as the potential for 51% attacks, reduced network security, and limited participation from smaller miners. We discuss the implications of centralization on the integrity and resilience of a blockchain network.

2. The Motivation for ASIC Resistance:

2.1 Preserving Decentralization: We discuss the fundamental principle of decentralization in blockchain networks and its importance in promoting trust, transparency, and censorship resistance. We highlight the need to preserve decentralization in the face of increasing ASIC dominance.

2.2 Fairness and Inclusion: We explore the concept of fairness in mining and the inclusion of a diverse range of participants. We discuss how ASIC resistance enables broader participation, levels the playing field, and prevents a mining monopoly.

3. Vertcoin's Approach to ASIC Resistance:

3.1 Technical Implementation of ASIC Resistance: We examine Vertcoin's technical implementation of ASIC resistance, including its choice of memory-intensive mining algorithms and regular algorithm changes. We discuss the rationale behind these measures and their effectiveness in deterring ASIC manufacturers.

3.2 Community Involvement and Consensus: We highlight the role of the Vertcoin community in supporting and driving ASIC resistance. We discuss the importance of consensus among stakeholders and the community's active involvement in decision-making processes.

4. Benefits of ASIC Resistance and Decentralization:

4.1 Enhancing Network Security: We explore how ASIC resistance enhances network security by preventing a single entity or a small group from acquiring majority control over the mining power. We discuss the resilience and robustness that decentralized mining brings to the Vertcoin network.

4.2 Fostering Innovation and Competition: We discuss how ASIC resistance fosters innovation and competition in the mining ecosystem. We examine how it encourages the development of alternative mining hardware and software solutions, leading to a more diverse and vibrant mining community.

5. Challenges and Criticisms:

5.1 Potential Trade-Offs and Efficiency Concerns: We address the criticisms and potential trade-offs associated with ASIC resistance, including concerns about mining efficiency and energy consumption. We discuss the ongoing debates surrounding the balance between decentralization and mining efficiency.

5.2 Adaptability and Network Consensus: We explore the challenges of maintaining ASIC resistance in the face of evolving technology and potential ASIC development. We discuss the importance of network consensus and community support in navigating these challenges.

6. Looking Ahead: The Future of ASIC Resistance and Decentralization:

6.1 Potential Impact on the Crypto Ecosystem: We speculate on the broader impact of ASIC resistance and decentralized mining on the crypto ecosystem. We discuss how the principles and practices championed by Vertcoin can influence the development of other cryptocurrencies and shape the industry as a whole.

6.2 Evolving Strategies and Innovations: We explore the potential for evolving strategies and innovations in ASIC resistance. We discuss the ongoing research and development efforts to enhance ASIC resistance and the role of Vertcoin as a pioneer in this space.

Conclusion:

In this concluding section of Chapter 4, we summarize the key aspects of the need for ASIC resistance and decentralization in the context of Vertcoin. We emphasize the importance of preserving decentralization, fairness, and inclusivity in cryptocurrency mining. We highlight the potential benefits of ASIC resistance and discuss the challenges and criticisms associated with this approach. We conclude by envisioning a future where ASIC resistance and decentralized mining play a crucial role in shaping a more resilient and democratic crypto ecosystem.

Vertcoin's Commitment to Fair Mining and Security

In this section, we explore Vertcoin's commitment to fair mining and security as a core principle of its peer-to-peer digital currency. We delve into the motivations behind Vertcoin's dedication to these aspects and examine the strategies and initiatives it has implemented to ensure fair mining practices and robust network security.

1. The Importance of Fair Mining:

1.1 Fair Distribution of Rewards: We discuss the significance of fair mining and its impact on the distribution of mining rewards. We examine the challenges associated with centralized mining and how it can lead to imbalances and concentration of power. We highlight Vertcoin's commitment to fair distribution and the benefits it brings to the mining community.

1.2 Leveling the Playing Field: We explore how Vertcoin's ASIC resistance contributes to fair mining by leveling the playing field for all participants. We discuss how this approach promotes inclusivity, encourages participation from smaller miners, and prevents mining monopolies.

2. Strategies for Fair Mining:

2.1 Memory-Intensive Mining Algorithms: We delve into Vertcoin's choice of memory-intensive mining algorithms, such as Lyra2REv3 and Verthash, and how they contribute to fair mining. We explain the technical aspects of these algorithms and their effectiveness in deterring specialized mining hardware.

2.2 Regular Algorithm Updates: We discuss Vertcoin's strategy of regular algorithm updates to maintain ASIC resistance and fair mining practices. We explore the benefits of algorithm changes and how they prevent the development of ASICs tailored for Vertcoin mining.

3. Network Security and Robustness:

3.1 Resilience Against 51% Attacks: We examine how Vertcoin's commitment to fair mining enhances network security and resilience against 51% attacks. We discuss the implications of a decentralized mining ecosystem on the integrity and trustworthiness of the blockchain.

3.2 Mitigating Double Spending and Sybil Attacks: We explore how fair mining practices contribute to mitigating double spending and Sybil attacks. We discuss the importance of network security measures and how Vertcoin's commitment to fair mining aligns with these objectives.

4. Community Engagement and Governance:

4.1 Community-Driven Development: We highlight the role of the Vertcoin community in shaping and maintaining fair mining practices. We discuss the community-driven development model and the participation of community members in decision-making processes.

4.2 Transparency and Accountability: We examine how Vertcoin promotes transparency and accountability in its governance and development. We discuss the open-source nature of the project and the visibility of its codebase, allowing the community to actively monitor and contribute to the project's progress.

5. Collaboration and Industry Impact:

5.1 Advocating for Fair Mining Standards: We explore Vertcoin's role in advocating for fair mining standards within the broader cryptocurrency industry. We discuss its collaboration with other projects and organizations to promote fair mining practices and raise awareness about the importance of decentralization.

5.2 Influencing the Crypto Ecosystem: We discuss how Vertcoin's commitment to fair mining and security can influence the wider crypto ecosystem. We examine the potential impact of its principles and practices on the development of other cryptocurrencies and the industry as a whole.

6. Challenges and Future Considerations:

6.1 Scalability and Efficiency: We address the challenges of scalability and efficiency in fair mining practices. We discuss the trade-offs between fair mining and the need for high transaction throughput, as well as potential solutions and innovations in this regard.

6.2 Continuous Improvement and Adaptability: We emphasize the importance of continuous improvement and adaptability in maintaining fair mining practices and network security. We discuss the need for ongoing research, development, and community engagement to address emerging challenges and ensure the long-term sustainability of Vertcoin's commitment to fair mining.

Conclusion:

In this concluding section, we summarize the key aspects of Vertcoin's commitment to fair mining and security. We highlight its dedication to maintaining a decentralized mining ecosystem, promoting inclusivity, and enhancing network security. We discuss the impact of fair mining on the broader crypto industry and emphasize the importance of continuous improvement and adaptation in ensuring the long-term success of Vertcoin's principles.

Adoption and Use Cases in the Crypto Landscape

In this section, we explore the adoption and use cases of Vertcoin in the wider crypto landscape. We delve into the factors that contribute to its adoption, the industries and communities that have embraced Vertcoin, and the practical applications that demonstrate its value as a peer-to-peer digital currency with ASIC resistance.

1. Early Adoption and Growth:

1.1 Early Adopters and Enthusiasts: We discuss the early adopters and enthusiasts who recognized the potential of Vertcoin and contributed to its initial growth. We highlight the community-driven nature of Vertcoin's adoption and how it fostered a dedicated user base.

1.2 Organic Growth and Community Support: We examine the role of community support in the organic growth of Vertcoin. We discuss the initiatives, events, and grassroots efforts that have helped spread awareness and attract new users to the Vertcoin ecosystem.

2. Merchant Adoption and E-commerce:

2.1 Online Retailers and Services: We explore the adoption of Vertcoin by online retailers and e-commerce platforms. We discuss the benefits of using Vertcoin for online transactions, such as low fees, fast confirmations, and enhanced security.

2.2 Micropayments and Content Monetization: We delve into the use of Vertcoin for micropayments and content monetization. We discuss how Vertcoin's low transaction fees and fast settlement times make it suitable for tipping, rewarding content creators, and supporting online communities.

3. Gaming and Virtual Economies:

3.1 Integration in Gaming Platforms: We examine the integration of Vertcoin in gaming platforms and virtual economies. We discuss the benefits of using Vertcoin as a digital currency for in-game purchases, virtual assets, and cross-platform transactions.

3.2 Enabling Player-to-Player Transactions: We explore how Vertcoin enables peer-to-peer transactions within gaming communities. We discuss the advantages of decentralized transactions, such as increased security, reduced fees, and greater control over virtual assets.

4. Decentralized Finance (DeFi) and Smart Contracts:

4.1 Vertcoin's Role in DeFi: We discuss the potential of Vertcoin in decentralized finance (DeFi) applications. We explore how Vertcoin's secure and decentralized nature can contribute to various DeFi use cases, such as lending, borrowing, and decentralized exchanges.

4.2 Smart Contract Platforms and Interoperability: We examine the role of Vertcoin in smart contract platforms and its interoperability with other blockchain networks. We discuss the potential for Vertcoin to facilitate cross-chain transactions and enable seamless interaction with smart contracts.

5. Community Projects and Innovations:

5.1 Vertcoin Development Fund (VDF): We highlight the Vertcoin Development Fund (VDF) and its role in supporting community-driven projects and innovations. We discuss the impact of the VDF on the Vertcoin ecosystem and the development of new features and technologies.

5.2 Partnerships and Collaborations: We explore the partnerships and collaborations that Vertcoin has formed with other projects and organizations. We discuss the synergies created through these partnerships and the potential for joint initiatives to expand the use cases of Vertcoin.

6. Future Prospects and Challenges:

6.1 Scalability and Mass Adoption: We address the scalability challenges and the potential for Vertcoin to achieve mass adoption. We discuss the ongoing research and development efforts to address scalability concerns and enhance the user experience.

6.2 Regulatory and Legal Considerations: We examine the regulatory and legal landscape surrounding Vertcoin and its implications for adoption. We discuss the challenges and opportunities presented by regulatory frameworks and the importance of compliance in fostering widespread acceptance.

Conclusion:

In this concluding section, we summarize the adoption and use cases of Vertcoin in the crypto landscape. We emphasize the growing acceptance of Vertcoin among various industries and communities, highlighting its role as a peer-to-peer digital currency with ASIC resistance. We discuss the future prospects of Vertcoin and the challenges it may face as it strives for further adoption and integration within the broader crypto ecosystem.

Chapter 5: SiaCoin (SC), established 2015 -

"Decentralized cloud storage platform."

Decentralized Cloud Storage Platform

In this section, we explore the concept of SiaCoin as a decentralized cloud storage platform. We delve into the underlying technology, principles, and benefits that make SiaCoin a unique solution for secure and efficient cloud storage.

1. Understanding Decentralized Cloud Storage:

1.1 Traditional Cloud Storage Challenges: We discuss the limitations and challenges associated with traditional cloud storage, including data security, privacy concerns, centralized control, and high costs. We highlight the need for an alternative solution that addresses these issues.

1.2 The Promise of Decentralization: We explain the concept of decentralization in cloud storage and how it addresses the shortcomings of centralized systems. We discuss the advantages of distributing data across a decentralized network and the benefits it offers in terms of security, privacy, and reliability.

2. The Technology Behind SiaCoin:

2.1 Sia's Blockchain-based Storage Solution: We delve into the technology behind SiaCoin, including its blockchain-based storage solution. We discuss how Sia utilizes smart contracts and encryption to enable secure and decentralized storage of data.

2.2 File Contracts and Storage Proof: We explain the process of file contracts in Sia and how they ensure the integrity and availability of stored data. We discuss the concept of storage proof and how it provides cryptographic evidence of data storage without relying on a centralized authority.

3. Security, Privacy, and Cost Efficiency:

3.1 Enhanced Data Security: We highlight the security features of SiaCoin, such as client-side encryption, data redundancy, and distributed storage. We discuss how these features protect user data from unauthorized access and potential breaches.

3.2 Privacy in Cloud Storage: We explore the privacy benefits of SiaCoin's decentralized cloud storage platform. We discuss how SiaCoin's architecture ensures that only the user has access to their data, preventing third-party surveillance and data mining.

3.3 Cost Efficiency and Fair Pricing: We discuss the cost advantages of using SiaCoin for cloud storage. We highlight how the decentralized nature of SiaCoin eliminates intermediaries, resulting in lower costs compared to traditional cloud storage providers. We also discuss the role of the SiaCoin marketplace in facilitating fair pricing and competition.

4. Real-world Applications and Adoption:

4.1 Enterprise Use Cases: We explore the potential use cases of SiaCoin in enterprise environments. We discuss how SiaCoin can benefit businesses in terms of secure data storage, backup solutions, and cost-effective scalability.

4.2 Personal and Consumer Applications: We discuss the practical applications of SiaCoin for individuals and consumers. We explore how SiaCoin can be used for personal data storage, file sharing, and collaboration, emphasizing the advantages of privacy and control over one's own data.

5. Future Development and Challenges:

5.1 Improving User Experience and Accessibility: We discuss the ongoing development efforts to enhance the user experience and accessibility of SiaCoin's decentralized cloud storage platform. We explore potential improvements in user interfaces, storage management tools, and integration with existing cloud storage solutions.

5.2 Scalability and Network Stability: We address the scalability challenges faced by SiaCoin and the efforts to ensure network stability as the platform grows. We discuss potential solutions, such as sharding and incentivizing network participants, to support a larger user base and accommodate increasing storage demands.

Conclusion:

In this concluding section, we summarize the key aspects of SiaCoin as a decentralized cloud storage platform. We highlight the advantages of its technology, including enhanced security, privacy, and cost efficiency. We discuss the real-world applications of SiaCoin and its potential to revolutionize the cloud storage industry. We also address the challenges and future prospects of SiaCoin as it continues to evolve and gain traction in the crypto and storage communities.

Exploring Sia's Blockchain-based Storage Solution

In this section, we dive deep into SiaCoin's innovative blockchain-based storage solution. We explore the underlying technology, the role of smart contracts, and the benefits it offers in terms of security, reliability, and cost-efficiency.

1. Understanding Sia's Blockchain-based Storage:

1.1 Introduction to Sia's Architecture: We provide an overview of Sia's architecture, explaining how it utilizes blockchain technology to create a decentralized storage network. We discuss the components involved, including hosts, renters, and the Sia blockchain.

1.2 Smart Contracts in Sia: We explore the concept of smart contracts within the Sia ecosystem. We explain how smart contracts are used to establish agreements between hosts and renters, ensuring the secure and reliable storage of data. We discuss the role of smart contracts in facilitating the negotiation, payment, and enforcement of storage agreements.

2. How Sia Ensures Security:

2.1 Client-side Encryption: We highlight one of the key security features of SiaCoin—the client-side encryption. We discuss how client-side encryption ensures that data remains encrypted throughout the storage process, providing an additional layer of security and privacy.

2.2 Redundancy and Data Integrity: We delve into Sia's approach to data redundancy and integrity. We explain how Sia utilizes redundancy techniques to store data across multiple hosts, mitigating the risk of data loss or corruption. We also discuss the mechanisms in place to ensure the integrity and authenticity of stored data.

3. The Storage Process on Sia:

3.1 File Uploading and Fragmentation: We walk through the process of uploading files to Sia's decentralized storage network. We explain how files are fragmented, encrypted, and distributed across multiple hosts, enhancing data security and availability.

3.2 Retrieving and Downloading Files: We discuss the retrieval and downloading process in Sia. We explore how the network retrieves and assembles file fragments from multiple hosts to reconstruct the original file for the renter.

4. Benefits of Sia's Storage Solution:

4.1 Enhanced Data Privacy: We emphasize the privacy advantages of Sia's blockchain-based storage solution. We explain how the decentralized nature of Sia ensures that only the renter has access to their data, minimizing the risk of unauthorized access or surveillance.

4.2 Reliability and Availability: We discuss how Sia's distributed storage model enhances data reliability and availability. We explain how the redundancy of data across multiple hosts ensures that files remain accessible even if some hosts go offline.

4.3 Cost Efficiency and Fair Pricing: We explore the cost advantages of using Sia for storage purposes. We discuss how Sia's decentralized model eliminates the need for intermediaries, resulting in lower storage costs compared to traditional cloud storage providers. We also highlight the role of the Sia marketplace in promoting fair pricing and competition among hosts.

5. Challenges and Future Development:

5.1 Scalability and Network Performance: We address the scalability challenges faced by Sia's blockchain-based storage solution. We discuss the efforts being made to improve network performance, such as optimization techniques and network upgrades, to accommodate increased demand and storage requirements.

5.2 User Experience and Accessibility: We discuss ongoing development efforts to enhance the user experience and accessibility of Sia's storage solution. We explore potential improvements in user interfaces, storage management tools, and integration with existing storage platforms.

Conclusion:

In this concluding section, we summarize the key aspects of Sia's blockchain-based storage solution. We highlight its use of smart contracts, client-side encryption, and data redundancy to ensure secure and reliable storage. We emphasize the benefits of enhanced data privacy, reliability, and cost efficiency offered by SiaCoin. Finally, we discuss the challenges and future development prospects for Sia's decentralized cloud storage platform, envisioning its potential to revolutionize the storage industry.

Security, Privacy, and Cost Efficiency Advantages

In this section, we delve into the security, privacy, and cost efficiency advantages offered by SiaCoin's decentralized cloud storage platform. We explore how Sia addresses common concerns in traditional cloud storage solutions and provides innovative solutions to ensure data security, privacy, and cost-effectiveness.

1. Ensuring Data Security:

1.1 Client-Side Encryption: We discuss how SiaCoin prioritizes data security through client-side encryption. We explain how client-side encryption ensures that data is encrypted locally on the user's device before it is uploaded to the Sia network, providing an additional layer of protection against unauthorized access.

1.2 Distributed Storage and Redundancy: We explore how Sia's decentralized storage model enhances data security. We discuss the concept of distributed storage, where data is fragmented and stored across multiple hosts. We explain how redundancy is achieved to safeguard against data loss or corruption.

1.3 Immutable Blockchain and Data Integrity: We highlight the role of the immutable blockchain in maintaining data integrity within Sia's storage platform. We discuss how the blockchain ensures the authenticity and verifiability of stored data, making it resistant to tampering or manipulation.

2. Preserving User Privacy:

2.1 Decentralized Architecture and User Control: We explain how SiaCoin's decentralized architecture contributes to user privacy. We discuss how users have full control over their data and are not reliant on centralized storage providers. We explore the advantages of decentralization in terms of limiting data exposure and protecting user privacy.

2.2 Encryption and Anonymity: We delve into the privacy features offered by SiaCoin, such as end-to-end encryption and anonymity. We discuss how Sia ensures that only the user has access to their data, preventing unauthorized access or surveillance.

2.3 Pseudonymous Transactions: We explore the pseudonymous nature of transactions within the Sia network. We explain how transactions are recorded on the blockchain without revealing the identities of the parties involved, adding an additional layer of privacy for users.

3. Cost Efficiency and Fair Pricing:

3.1 Eliminating Intermediaries: We discuss how Sia's decentralized model eliminates intermediaries typically found in traditional cloud storage solutions. We explain how this eliminates additional costs associated with intermediaries and results in more cost-efficient storage options for users.

3.2 Competitive Marketplace: We explore the role of the Sia marketplace in promoting fair pricing and competition among hosts. We discuss how the marketplace encourages hosts to offer competitive pricing, allowing users to choose storage options that best fit their budget and requirements.

3.3 Microtransactions and Payment Flexibility: We highlight the use of microtransactions in SiaCoin, enabling users to pay for storage on a pay-as-you-go basis. We discuss the advantages of this flexible payment system, allowing users to scale their storage needs and minimize upfront costs.

4. Challenges and Future Development:

4.1 Scalability and Network Performance: We address the scalability challenges faced by SiaCoin's decentralized storage platform. We discuss ongoing development efforts to enhance network performance and accommodate growing storage demands.

4.2 Usability and User Experience: We explore the challenges related to usability and user experience in decentralized storage platforms. We discuss the importance of intuitive interfaces and user-friendly tools to facilitate broader adoption of SiaCoin.

Conclusion:

In this concluding section, we summarize the security, privacy, and cost efficiency advantages offered by SiaCoin's decentralized cloud storage platform. We highlight the significance of client-side encryption, distributed storage, and blockchain immutability in ensuring data security. We emphasize the privacy benefits of decentralized architecture, encryption, and pseudonymous transactions. Finally, we discuss the cost efficiency achieved through the elimination of intermediaries, competitive pricing, and flexible payment options. We acknowledge the challenges faced by SiaCoin and speculate on its future development, envisioning its potential to transform the cloud storage industry.

Real-world Applications and Future Development

In this section, we explore the real-world applications of SiaCoin's decentralized cloud storage platform and delve into its future development. We discuss how SiaCoin has the potential to revolutionize various industries by offering secure, private, and cost-effective storage solutions. We also examine the ongoing advancements and innovations within the Sia ecosystem that contribute to its growth and adoption.

1. Real-world Applications:

1.1 Personal Cloud Storage: We discuss how SiaCoin can be used as a personal cloud storage solution. We explore the advantages of storing personal data on the decentralized Sia network, such as enhanced security, privacy, and control over data. We highlight the ease of use and convenience offered by Sia's user-friendly interfaces for personal storage needs.

1.2 Enterprise Data Storage: We delve into the potential applications of SiaCoin in enterprise data storage. We discuss how businesses can leverage the secure and cost-efficient storage infrastructure provided by Sia to store sensitive data, backups, and archives. We explore the benefits of decentralization in mitigating data breaches and reducing reliance on traditional cloud storage providers.

1.3 Decentralized Applications (dApps): We explore how SiaCoin can support decentralized applications (dApps). We discuss the integration of Sia's storage capabilities with various dApps, such as decentralized file-sharing platforms, content delivery networks (CDNs), and blockchain-based storage solutions. We highlight the advantages of utilizing Sia's decentralized infrastructure for data-intensive dApps.

1.4 Content Distribution and Streaming: We examine the potential of SiaCoin in content distribution and streaming services. We discuss how Sia's distributed storage model can improve the delivery of large media files, reduce latency, and enhance scalability. We explore the implications of using Sia for video streaming, content hosting, and media distribution.

2. Future Development:

2.1 Network Scalability and Performance: We discuss the ongoing efforts to improve the scalability and performance of the Sia network. We explore the implementation of technologies such as sharding, off-chain solutions, and network optimizations to accommodate growing storage demands and ensure smooth operation.

2.2 Interoperability and Integration: We explore the potential for SiaCoin to integrate with other blockchain projects and storage protocols. We discuss the importance of interoperability in expanding the reach of Sia and enabling seamless data exchange between different decentralized storage networks. We explore partnerships and collaborations that can further enhance Sia's capabilities.

2.3 User Experience and Interface Enhancements: We discuss the focus on improving the user experience and interface of SiaCoin. We explore the development of user-friendly tools, intuitive interfaces, and mobile applications to attract a broader user base. We discuss the importance of simplifying the onboarding process and ensuring a seamless user experience.

2.4 Integration with Web 3.0 and Decentralized Web: We explore the integration of SiaCoin with the concept of Web 3.0 and the decentralized web. We discuss how Sia's decentralized storage can contribute to the vision of a more open, censorship-resistant, and privacy-focused internet. We explore the potential synergies between Sia and other projects working towards a decentralized web infrastructure.

Conclusion:

In this concluding section, we summarize the real-world applications of SiaCoin's decentralized cloud storage platform, ranging from personal storage to enterprise data management and dApp integration. We emphasize the advantages of Sia in terms of security, privacy, and cost efficiency for various use cases. We highlight the ongoing developments in the Sia ecosystem, including network scalability, interoperability, user experience enhancements, and integration with the decentralized web. We envision a future where SiaCoin plays a significant role in shaping the landscape of decentralized storage and revolutionizing the way we store and manage data.

Chapter 6: Comparative Analysis and Synergies Contrasting the Unique Characteristics of the Featured Coins

In this section, we delve into a comparative analysis of the featured coins: Ixcoin (IXC), Freicoin (FRC), Dogecoin (DOGE), Vertcoin (VTC), and SiaCoin (SC). We explore the unique characteristics and attributes of each coin, highlighting their strengths and differences. By contrasting these coins, we gain a deeper understanding of their contributions to the cryptocurrency ecosystem and identify potential synergies among them.

1. Ixcoin (IXC):

1.1 Global Decentralized Currency: We discuss how Ixcoin aims to serve as a global decentralized currency. We explore its origins, the underlying technology, and its vision for a decentralized financial system. We highlight Ixcoin's emphasis on security, transaction speed, and its goal of becoming a widely adopted medium of exchange.

1.2 Community Governance and Consensus Mechanisms: We examine Ixcoin's community governance model and consensus mechanisms. We discuss the role of stakeholders in decision-making and the consensus algorithm used by Ixcoin. We contrast Ixcoin's governance model with other featured coins to understand its unique approach to community involvement and decentralized decision-making.

1.3 Adoption and Use Cases: We explore the adoption and use cases of Ixcoin. We discuss its acceptance by merchants, businesses, and individuals as a form of payment. We examine the sectors where Ixcoin is being utilized and its potential for financial inclusion in underserved regions. We highlight the challenges and opportunities in Ixcoin's path to mainstream adoption.

2. Freicoin (FRC):

2.1 Demurrage Currency with Distribution Mechanisms: We delve into the concept of demurrage currency and its purpose in Freicoin. We explain how Freicoin's demurrage feature encourages circulation and discourages hoarding. We discuss the distribution mechanisms employed by Freicoin to ensure a fair and equitable distribution of currency.

2.2 Economic and Social Impact: We analyze the economic and social impact of Freicoin's demurrage currency. We discuss its potential to stimulate economic activity, promote sustainable consumption, and reduce wealth inequality. We contrast Freicoin's economic model with traditional fiat currencies and explore the advantages and challenges it presents.

2.3 Adoption and Implementation Challenges: We examine the challenges faced by Freicoin in terms of adoption and implementation. We discuss the barriers to widespread acceptance and the resistance encountered due to the unconventional nature of its economic model. We explore the potential synergies between Freicoin and other alternative currency systems.

3. Dogecoin (DOGE):

3.1 The Fun and Friendly Internet Currency: We explore Dogecoin's unique positioning as the fun and friendly internet currency. We discuss its origins as a meme-based cryptocurrency and its rapid rise in popularity. We analyze the cultural impact of Dogecoin and its ability to engage a broad user base, including the role of social media and online communities.

3.2 Community-driven Initiatives and Philanthropy: We delve into Dogecoin's community-driven initiatives and philanthropic endeavors. We discuss the notable charitable campaigns supported by Dogecoin and its community's ethos of giving back. We contrast Dogecoin's philanthropic culture with other cryptocurrencies and explore the potential for community-driven impact.

3.3 Technological Advancements and Future Potential: We examine the technological advancements and future potential of Dogecoin. We discuss its transition from a meme to a viable cryptocurrency, including recent developments such as protocol upgrades and scalability improvements. We analyze the challenges and opportunities in Dogecoin's path to long-term sustainability and innovation.

4. Vertcoin (VTC):

4.1 Peer-to-Peer Digital Currency with ASIC Resistance: We explore Vertcoin's positioning as a peer-to-peer digital currency with a focus on ASIC resistance. We explain the concept of ASIC resistance and its importance in maintaining decentralization and fair mining practices. We discuss Vertcoin's commitment to empowering individual miners and ensuring a level playing field.

4.2 Decentralized Governance and Community Involvement: We examine Vertcoin's decentralized governance model and community involvement. We discuss the role of stakeholders in decision-making and the mechanisms for consensus building within the Vertcoin community. We contrast Vertcoin's governance approach with other featured coins to understand its unique characteristics.

4.3 Adoption and Use Cases in the Crypto Landscape: We explore the adoption and use cases of Vertcoin in the broader cryptocurrency landscape. We discuss its acceptance by merchants, its integration with existing payment systems, and its potential for use in decentralized applications. We analyze the challenges and opportunities in Vertcoin's pursuit of broader adoption and utility.

5. SiaCoin (SC):

5.1 Decentralized Cloud Storage Platform: We delve into SiaCoin's role as a decentralized cloud storage platform. We discuss its underlying technology, including blockchain and smart contracts, and how it enables secure and private storage of data. We explore the advantages of decentralized storage and its potential to disrupt traditional cloud storage solutions.

5.2 Security, Privacy, and Cost Efficiency Advantages: We analyze the security, privacy, and cost efficiency advantages offered by SiaCoin's decentralized storage platform. We discuss the use of encryption, data redundancy, and distributed networks to ensure data integrity and protection. We contrast SiaCoin's model with centralized cloud storage providers to highlight its unique value proposition.

5.3 Real-world Applications and Future Development: We examine the real-world applications of SiaCoin's decentralized storage platform. We discuss its potential use cases across various industries, such as data backup, file sharing, and content distribution. We explore the challenges and opportunities in SiaCoin's journey towards widespread adoption and scalability.

Conclusion:

By contrasting the unique characteristics of Ixcoin, Freicoin, Dogecoin, Vertcoin, and SiaCoin, we gain a comprehensive understanding of their contributions to the cryptocurrency ecosystem. We highlight their distinct features, adoption challenges, community-driven initiatives, and future prospects. Moreover, we identify potential synergies among these coins, paving the way for collaboration and innovation in the evolving landscape of decentralized finance and digital currencies.

Identifying Synergies and Potential Collaborations

In this section, we explore the comparative analysis of the featured coins: Ixcoin (IXC), Freicoin (FRC), Dogecoin (DOGE), Vertcoin (VTC), and SiaCoin (SC). Building upon our understanding of their unique characteristics, we now delve into identifying synergies and potential collaborations among these coins. By recognizing shared goals, complementary features, and collaborative opportunities, we can unlock the power of collective innovation and foster a more robust cryptocurrency ecosystem.

1. Shared Principles and Objectives:

1.1 Decentralization and Community Empowerment: We examine how all featured coins share a common commitment to decentralization and community empowerment. We discuss the importance of these principles in fostering trust, resilience, and inclusivity within the cryptocurrency ecosystem. We explore potential avenues for collaboration in community governance, consensus mechanisms, and decentralized decision-making.

1.2 Financial Inclusion and Accessibility: We highlight the shared objective of promoting financial inclusion and accessibility. We discuss how each coin seeks to provide an alternative financial system that is accessible to individuals and communities globally. We explore potential collaborations in bridging the gap between traditional financial systems and emerging decentralized economies.

2. Complementary Features and Technologies:

2.1 Interoperability and Cross-chain Solutions: We explore the potential for interoperability and cross-chain solutions among the featured coins. We discuss the advantages of seamless transferability of assets and data across different blockchain networks. We examine potential collaborations in developing interoperability protocols and facilitating cross-chain transactions.

2.2 Privacy and Security Enhancements: We analyze the privacy and security features offered by each coin. We discuss techniques such as zero-knowledge proofs, advanced encryption, and data obfuscation. We explore potential collaborations in enhancing privacy and security standards across the cryptocurrency ecosystem, ensuring the protection of user data and transactions.

2.3 Scalability and Transaction Speed: We delve into the scalability and transaction speed challenges faced by cryptocurrencies. We discuss the various approaches taken by the featured coins to address these issues, such as layer 2 solutions, sharding, and off-chain transactions. We explore potential collaborations in developing scalable solutions that can benefit the entire ecosystem.

3. Collaborative Use Cases and Applications:

3.1 Cross-border Payments and Remittances: We explore the potential for collaborative solutions in cross-border payments and remittances. We discuss the challenges associated with traditional payment systems and how blockchain-based solutions can provide faster, more cost-effective, and secure cross-border transactions. We explore potential partnerships and integrations among the featured coins.

3.2 Decentralized Applications and Smart Contracts: We discuss the potential for collaborative efforts in developing decentralized applications (DApps) and smart contracts. We explore the unique features and capabilities of each coin's underlying blockchain technology and identify areas where collaboration can enhance the functionality and utility of DApps and smart contract ecosystems.

3.3 Sustainable and Green Blockchain Solutions: We highlight the importance of sustainability and environmental consciousness in the cryptocurrency ecosystem. We discuss the energy consumption challenges associated with proof-of-work consensus algorithms and the potential for collaborative efforts in developing energy-efficient and environmentally friendly blockchain solutions. We explore the shared objective of minimizing the ecological footprint of blockchain technology.

Conclusion:

Through a comprehensive comparative analysis of the featured coins, we have identified synergies and potential collaborations that can drive innovation and advancement within the cryptocurrency ecosystem. By leveraging shared principles, complementary features, and collaborative use cases, these coins can collectively address challenges, unlock new possibilities, and create a more robust and inclusive financial landscape. Collaboration among Ixcoin, Freicoin, Dogecoin, Vertcoin, and SiaCoin has the potential to set the stage for transformative advancements in decentralized finance and shape the future of digital currencies.

Examining the Broader Impact of PoW Coins in the Crypto Industry

In this section, we delve into the broader impact of Proof-of-Work (PoW) coins in the cryptocurrency industry. As we have explored the unique characteristics and synergies among the featured coins, it is essential to understand their significance within the larger crypto landscape. We analyze the contributions of PoW coins to various aspects of the industry, including technology development, market dynamics, and community engagement. By examining their impact, we can gain a comprehensive understanding of the role and importance of PoW coins in shaping the future of cryptocurrencies.

1. Technological Advancements and Innovation:

1.1 Consensus Mechanisms and Security: We examine how PoW coins have played a crucial role in advancing consensus mechanisms and enhancing network security. We discuss the evolution of PoW algorithms, their resistance to attacks, and their contribution to the overall security of blockchain networks. We explore the ongoing research and development efforts to improve PoW algorithms and their potential impact on the industry.

1.2 Scalability Solutions: We analyze the challenges of scalability faced by PoW coins and the innovative solutions that have emerged. We discuss layer 2 protocols, off-chain transactions, and other scalability techniques implemented by PoW coins. We explore the impact of these solutions on the broader crypto industry and their potential for further development and adoption.

1.3 Privacy and Confidentiality Enhancements: We explore how PoW coins have contributed to privacy and confidentiality advancements in the crypto industry. We discuss the integration of privacy-centric features, such as zero-knowledge proofs and ring signatures, into PoW coin protocols. We examine the impact of these enhancements on user privacy and the potential for wider adoption of privacy-focused cryptocurrencies.

2. Market Dynamics and Financial Landscape:

2.1 Market Influence and Price Volatility: We analyze the influence of PoW coins on the overall cryptocurrency market and their role in price volatility. We discuss the market dynamics driven by mining activities, coin supply, and investor sentiment. We explore the impact of PoW coins' market movements on the broader crypto ecosystem and the challenges and opportunities they present.

2.2 Trading and Exchanges: We examine the role of PoW coins in facilitating trading activities and their integration into cryptocurrency exchanges. We discuss the liquidity and trading volume generated by PoW coins and their impact on the overall trading ecosystem. We explore the challenges faced by PoW coins in terms of listing, market access, and regulatory compliance.

2.3 Investment and Funding Opportunities: We explore the investment and funding opportunities provided by PoW coins. We discuss initial coin offerings (ICOs), token sales, and fundraising initiatives launched by PoW projects. We analyze the impact of these funding mechanisms on the industry and the potential for innovative projects to secure capital through PoW-based fundraising.

3. Community Engagement and Adoption:

3.1 Developer Communities and Ecosystem Growth: We examine the role of PoW coins in fostering vibrant developer communities and ecosystem growth. We discuss how PoW coins have attracted developers to contribute to their projects, build decentralized applications, and enhance the overall ecosystem. We explore the impact of community engagement on the success and adoption of PoW coins.

3.2 User Adoption and Real-world Applications: We analyze the user adoption of PoW coins and their real-world applications. We discuss the challenges and opportunities in promoting mainstream adoption of PoW-based cryptocurrencies as a medium of exchange, store of value, or investment vehicle. We explore the impact of user adoption on the broader acceptance and utility of PoW coins.

3.3 Regulatory Considerations and Compliance: We examine the regulatory landscape surrounding PoW coins and their impact on industry compliance. We discuss the challenges faced by PoW coins in terms of regulatory clarity, anti-money laundering (AML) measures, and know-your-customer (KYC) requirements. We explore the potential for regulatory frameworks to shape the future of PoW coins and their wider acceptance.

Conclusion:

In this section, we have examined the broader impact of PoW coins in the cryptocurrency industry. We have explored their contributions to technological advancements, market dynamics, and community engagement. By understanding the impact of PoW coins, we gain insights into their significance within the crypto industry and their potential for future growth and development. As the industry continues to evolve, PoW coins will play a vital role in shaping the future of cryptocurrencies.

Chapter 7: Shaping the Future of Blockchain Evaluating the Role of PoW Coins in the Advancement of Blockchain Technology

In this section, we evaluate the significant role of Proof-of-Work (PoW) coins in advancing blockchain technology. As we have explored the individual characteristics and contributions of PoW coins, it is crucial to assess their collective impact on the broader development and adoption of blockchain. We analyze how PoW coins have driven innovation, scalability, security, and decentralization in blockchain technology. By evaluating their role, we can gain insights into the future trajectory of blockchain and the continued evolution of PoW coins.

1. Innovation and Technological Advancements:

1.1 Consensus Mechanisms and Distributed Ledger Technology: We evaluate how PoW coins have contributed to the innovation and evolution of consensus mechanisms. We discuss the strengths and limitations of PoW as a consensus algorithm and its impact on the development of distributed ledger technology. We explore alternative consensus mechanisms and their potential to enhance blockchain scalability, energy efficiency, and transaction throughput.

1.2 Smart Contracts and Decentralized Applications (DApps): We assess the role of PoW coins in the advancement of smart contract platforms and the proliferation of decentralized applications (DApps). We analyze the impact of PoW coins in enabling programmable blockchain ecosystems and the potential for DApps to revolutionize various industries. We discuss the challenges and opportunities in scaling smart contract platforms and their significance in the future of blockchain technology.

1.3 Interoperability and Cross-Chain Solutions: We evaluate how PoW coins have contributed to interoperability and cross-chain solutions in the blockchain ecosystem. We discuss the challenges faced by different blockchains in achieving seamless communication and data transfer. We explore the role of PoW coins in fostering interoperability protocols and their potential to enable cross-chain transactions, asset transfers, and data sharing.

2. Scalability and Performance Enhancement:

2.1 Layer 2 Solutions and Off-Chain Scaling: We assess the impact of PoW coins on scalability through the implementation of layer 2 solutions and off-chain scaling techniques. We discuss the Lightning Network, state channels, and other layer 2 protocols that enable faster and more cost-effective transactions. We analyze the potential of these solutions to address the scalability limitations of PoW-based blockchains.

2.2 Sharding and Partitioning: We evaluate the role of PoW coins in exploring sharding and partitioning techniques to improve blockchain scalability. We discuss how PoW coins are experimenting with these approaches to enable parallel processing of transactions and data. We analyze the challenges and opportunities in implementing sharding and partitioning in PoW-based blockchains and their potential to enhance performance.

2.3 Sidechains and Cross-Chain Communication: We assess the impact of PoW coins in facilitating sidechain development and cross-chain communication. We discuss how PoW coins are leveraging sidechains to offload transactions and improve scalability while maintaining security. We explore the potential of cross-chain communication protocols to enable interoperability between different PoW-based blockchains.

3. Security and Decentralization:

3.1 Robust Network Security: We evaluate the role of PoW coins in providing robust network security for blockchain systems. We discuss how PoW-based blockchains leverage computational power to protect against attacks, including 51% attacks and double-spending. We explore the trade-offs between security and energy consumption and discuss potential enhancements to strengthen network security.

3.2 Decentralization and Governance: We assess the impact of PoW coins in promoting decentralization and community governance within blockchain networks. We discuss the role of miners in securing the network and the potential for decentralized governance models to ensure transparency and fairness. We analyze the challenges and opportunities in achieving true decentralization and effective governance in PoW-based blockchains.

3.3 Synergies with Other Consensus Mechanisms: We explore the potential synergies between PoW coins and other consensus mechanisms such as Proof-of-Stake (PoS) and Delegated Proof-of-Stake (DPoS). We evaluate the benefits of hybrid consensus models that combine the strengths of different algorithms. We discuss the potential for PoW coins to collaborate with other consensus mechanisms and enhance overall blockchain security and decentralization.

Conclusion:

In this section, we have evaluated the role of PoW coins in the advancement of blockchain technology. We have explored their contributions to innovation, scalability, security, and decentralization. By understanding their impact, we gain insights into the future of blockchain and the potential for PoW coins to shape the evolution of this transformative technology. As blockchain continues to mature, PoW coins will play a crucial role in driving its development, adoption, and overall impact on various industries.

Emerging Trends and Innovations

In this section, we explore the emerging trends and innovations that are shaping the future of blockchain technology. As blockchain continues to evolve, new ideas, technologies, and use cases are emerging, driving the next wave of innovation in the industry. We examine the key trends and innovations that are transforming the blockchain landscape and discuss their potential impact on various sectors.

1. Interoperability and Cross-Chain Solutions:

1.1 Interoperability Protocols: We delve into the growing importance of interoperability in blockchain networks. We discuss the emergence of interoperability protocols and their role in enabling seamless communication and data transfer between different blockchains. We explore projects such as Polkadot, Cosmos, and ICON that aim to bridge the gap between disparate blockchain networks and facilitate cross-chain transactions.

1.2 Cross-Chain Asset Transfers: We analyze the trend of cross-chain asset transfers and their potential to revolutionize the way digital assets are exchanged between blockchains. We discuss technologies like atomic swaps and decentralized exchanges (DEXs) that enable trustless and secure cross-chain transactions. We explore the benefits and challenges associated with cross-chain asset transfers and their implications for liquidity and market efficiency.

1.3 Cross-Chain Data Sharing: We explore the emerging trend of cross-chain data sharing and its potential to enable secure and decentralized access to data across multiple blockchain networks. We discuss the concept of oracle networks and how they facilitate the exchange of real-world data on the blockchain. We examine the challenges and opportunities in implementing cross-chain data sharing solutions and their applications in sectors such as supply chain management, finance, and healthcare.

2. Scalability Solutions:

2.1 Layer 2 Scaling Solutions: We delve into the various layer 2 scaling solutions that are being developed to address the scalability limitations of blockchain networks. We discuss technologies like state channels, payment channels, and sidechains that enable off-chain processing of transactions, reducing the burden on the main blockchain. We analyze the benefits and challenges of layer 2 scaling solutions and their potential to enhance blockchain throughput and user experience.

2.2 Sharding and Partitioning: We explore the trend of sharding and partitioning in blockchain networks as a means to achieve horizontal scalability. We discuss how these techniques divide the blockchain into smaller, more manageable parts, allowing for parallel processing of transactions and data. We analyze the benefits and challenges of sharding and partitioning and their potential to significantly increase blockchain scalability.

2.3 Optimized Consensus Algorithms: We examine the development of optimized consensus algorithms that aim to improve the scalability of blockchain networks. We discuss algorithms like Proof-of-Stake (PoS), Delegated Proof-of-Stake (DPoS), and Practical Byzantine Fault Tolerance (PBFT) that offer higher transaction throughput and energy efficiency compared to traditional Proof-of-Work (PoW) algorithms. We explore the trade-offs and challenges associated with these consensus algorithms and their potential impact on blockchain scalability.

3. Privacy and Confidentiality Solutions:

3.1 Zero-Knowledge Proofs and Privacy Coins: We delve into the emerging trend of zero-knowledge proofs (ZKPs) and privacy coins that aim to enhance privacy and confidentiality in blockchain transactions. We discuss how ZKPs enable verifiable computations without revealing sensitive information and how privacy coins provide enhanced anonymity for users. We explore the applications of privacy solutions in sectors such as finance, healthcare, and identity management.

3.2 Secure Multi-Party Computation: We explore the concept of secure multi-party computation (MPC) and its potential to enable privacy-preserving data analysis and computation on the blockchain. We discuss how MPC allows multiple parties to jointly perform computations on encrypted data without revealing the underlying data to each other. We analyze the benefits and challenges of secure MPC and its applications in areas like decentralized finance (DeFi) and data sharing.

3.3 Confidential Smart Contracts: We discuss the development of confidential smart contracts that enable the execution of private and secure transactions on the blockchain. We explore technologies like zero-knowledge smart contracts and secure enclaves that protect the confidentiality of contract inputs, outputs, and execution logic. We examine the potential use cases of confidential smart contracts in areas such as supply chain management, intellectual property, and decentralized applications (dApps).

4. Governance and Decentralized Autonomous Organizations (DAOs):

4.1 On-Chain Governance: We examine the emergence of on-chain governance models that enable stakeholders to participate in decision-making processes directly on the blockchain. We discuss the advantages and challenges of on-chain governance and its potential to enhance transparency, accountability, and community involvement in blockchain projects. We analyze different on-chain governance mechanisms and their implementations in prominent blockchain platforms.

4.2 Decentralized Autonomous Organizations (DAOs): We explore the concept of decentralized autonomous organizations (DAOs) and their potential to revolutionize traditional organizational structures. We discuss how DAOs leverage smart contracts and blockchain technology to enable decentralized decision-making and governance. We examine the challenges and opportunities in implementing DAOs and their applications in areas such as decentralized finance, governance, and collective decision-making.

Conclusion:

In this section, we have explored the emerging trends and innovations that are shaping the future of blockchain technology. Interoperability, scalability, privacy, and governance are key areas where significant advancements are being made. These trends and innovations have the potential to unlock new possibilities for blockchain adoption across various industries and pave the way for a more inclusive, scalable, and secure decentralized future. As the blockchain ecosystem continues to evolve, it is crucial to stay updated on these emerging trends to understand the evolving landscape and the opportunities they present for individuals, businesses, and society as a whole.

Speculating on the Future of PoW Coins and Their Impact on the Digital Economy

In this section, we delve into the future of Proof-of-Work (PoW) coins and their potential impact on the digital economy. While the blockchain industry is rapidly evolving, PoW remains a prominent consensus mechanism that has shaped the development of cryptocurrencies. We analyze the current state of PoW coins, explore their strengths and weaknesses, and speculate on their future trajectory. Furthermore, we discuss how PoW coins can contribute to the digital economy and the challenges they might face along the way.

1. The Evolution of PoW Coins:

1.1 Historical Perspective: We provide a historical overview of PoW coins, tracing their origins from the inception of Bitcoin to the present day. We highlight the key milestones, innovations, and challenges faced by PoW coins throughout their journey. This retrospective analysis sets the stage for understanding their future prospects.

1.2 Technical Advancements: We discuss the technical advancements that have occurred in PoW coins, including improvements in mining algorithms, network scalability, security, and transaction speed. We examine the emergence of alternative PoW algorithms, such as Equihash, Ethash, and RandomX, and their impact on decentralization, energy efficiency, and resistance to specialized mining hardware.

1.3 Governance and Community Development: We explore the governance models and community-driven development processes that shape PoW coins. We examine the role of miners, developers, and token holders in decision-making and consensus-building. Additionally, we discuss the challenges and opportunities associated with decentralized governance and the potential impact on the long-term viability of PoW coins.

2. PoW Coins in the Digital Economy:

2.1 Store of Value: We analyze the role of PoW coins as a store of value within the digital economy. We explore the attributes that make PoW coins attractive for wealth preservation and hedging against inflation. We discuss the potential of PoW coins to serve as a reliable store of value in comparison to traditional assets and other cryptocurrency alternatives.

2.2 Medium of Exchange: We examine the viability of PoW coins as a medium of exchange in day-to-day transactions. We discuss the challenges and opportunities of using PoW coins for everyday payments, including scalability, transaction speed, and user experience. We analyze the efforts made by PoW projects to enhance their payment capabilities and partnerships with merchants and payment processors.

2.3 Financial Services and DeFi: We explore the role of PoW coins in the emerging field of decentralized finance (DeFi). We discuss how PoW coins can facilitate lending, borrowing, staking, and other financial services within the DeFi ecosystem. We analyze the potential for PoW coins to provide a more inclusive and transparent financial system that reduces the reliance on traditional intermediaries.

3. Challenges and Future Prospects:

3.1 Scalability and Transaction Throughput: We address the scalability challenges faced by PoW coins, including network congestion and limited transaction throughput. We discuss the potential solutions, such as layer 2 scaling solutions, sharding, and off-chain transactions, that can alleviate these challenges and enable PoW coins to handle a higher volume of transactions.

3.2 Energy Consumption and Environmental Impact: We examine the concerns surrounding the energy consumption and environmental impact of PoW mining. We discuss the efforts made by PoW projects to improve energy efficiency and explore alternative energy sources, such as renewable energy, for powering mining operations. We analyze the potential for PoW coins to transition towards more sustainable mining practices.

3.3 Regulatory and Legal Considerations: We discuss the regulatory and legal considerations that PoW coins face in different jurisdictions. We analyze the impact of regulatory frameworks on the adoption and growth of PoW coins and the potential challenges they pose to their future development. We also explore the potential for regulatory clarity and favorable environments to foster the growth of PoW coins.

Conclusion:

In this section, we have speculated on the future of PoW coins and their impact on the digital economy. While PoW coins face challenges in scalability, energy consumption, and regulatory scrutiny, they continue to play a significant role in the blockchain ecosystem. With ongoing technical advancements and community-driven development, PoW coins have the potential to evolve and adapt to meet the demands of the digital economy. It is essential for stakeholders to closely monitor these developments and consider the implications for their investment strategies, business models, and the broader digital ecosystem.

Conclusion

Reflecting on the Contributions of PoW Coins Explored in Book 3

In this final section of Book 3, we take a moment to reflect on the contributions of Proof-of-Work (PoW) coins that have been explored throughout our journey. We revisit the key insights and learnings gained from examining the unique characteristics, use cases, challenges, and future prospects of each featured PoW coin. By summarizing these contributions, we can gain a comprehensive understanding of the significance and impact of PoW coins in the broader cryptocurrency landscape.

1. Recapitulating the Featured PoW Coins:

1.1 Ixcoin (IXC): We revisit the establishment of Ixcoin as a global decentralized currency in 2011. We reflect on its key attributes, including its blockchain-based infrastructure, security features, and decentralized governance model. We highlight the role of Ixcoin in providing an alternative means of value transfer and its potential to foster financial inclusion in underserved regions.

1.2 Freicoin (FRC): We recapitulate the concept of Freicoin as a demurrage currency with distribution mechanisms. We discuss the purpose of demurrage and its potential to stimulate economic activity, discourage hoarding, and promote fair wealth distribution. We reflect on the challenges faced by Freicoin and its potential for wider adoption as an alternative monetary system.

1.3 Dogecoin (DOGE): We revisit Dogecoin's journey from a meme to a mainstream internet currency. We reflect on its friendly and inclusive community, its philanthropic initiatives, and its role in promoting digital currency awareness. We analyze the impact of Dogecoin's cultural significance and its potential to bridge the gap between cryptocurrency and the general public.

1.4 Vertcoin (VTC): We recapitulate the establishment of Vertcoin as a peer-to-peer digital currency with ASIC resistance. We reflect on the importance of decentralization and its impact on network security, censorship resistance, and community engagement. We discuss Vertcoin's commitment to fair mining and its potential as a viable alternative to centralized digital currencies.

1.5 SiaCoin (SC): We revisit SiaCoin's role as a decentralized cloud storage platform. We reflect on its blockchain-based storage solution, emphasizing its security, privacy, and cost efficiency advantages. We analyze the potential use cases of SiaCoin in various industries and its contribution to the evolution of cloud storage and data management.

2. Evaluating the Collective Impact:

2.1 Technological Advancements: We evaluate the technological advancements made by PoW coins collectively. We discuss the innovations in mining algorithms, network scalability, security protocols, and transaction speed. We reflect on the impact of these advancements on the broader blockchain ecosystem and their potential to shape the future of decentralized applications and services.

2.2 Financial Inclusion and Economic Empowerment: We assess the collective contribution of PoW coins in fostering financial inclusion and empowering individuals in underserved communities. We reflect on their potential to provide accessible financial services, facilitate cross-border transactions, and reduce reliance on traditional intermediaries. We discuss the challenges and opportunities for PoW coins to drive economic empowerment globally.

2.3 Cultural Influence and Community Engagement: We analyze the collective cultural influence of PoW coins, particularly in fostering vibrant and engaged communities. We reflect on the philanthropic initiatives, community-driven projects, and collaborative efforts that have emerged around PoW coins. We discuss the potential for these communities to drive social change, promote digital literacy, and shape the future of the cryptocurrency ecosystem.

3. Looking Ahead: Future Perspectives:

3.1 Continued Evolution and Innovation: We speculate on the future evolution and innovation of PoW coins. We reflect on the challenges they may face, including scalability, energy consumption, regulatory scrutiny, and technological advancements. We discuss the potential for PoW coins to adapt and overcome these challenges through community-driven development, technological breakthroughs, and collaborations with other blockchain platforms.

3.2 Collaborative Synergies: We explore the potential for collaborative synergies among PoW coins and other blockchain projects. We discuss the opportunities for interoperability, cross-chain solutions, and shared resources that can enhance the overall functionality and utility of PoW coins. We reflect on the potential collaborations that could drive innovation, improve scalability, and address common challenges faced by PoW coins.

3.3 Impact on the Digital Economy: We assess the broader impact of PoW coins on the digital economy. We discuss their influence on financial systems, traditional industries, and emerging sectors such as decentralized finance (DeFi) and non-fungible tokens (NFTs). We reflect on the potential for PoW coins to reshape economic models, redefine ownership structures, and foster new business opportunities.

Conclusion:

In conclusion, the exploration of PoW coins in Book 3 has provided valuable insights into their unique characteristics, use cases, challenges, and future prospects. We have reflected on the contributions of each featured coin, evaluating their impact on financial inclusion, cultural influence, technological advancements, and the broader digital economy. By understanding the collective impact of PoW coins, we can envision a future where decentralized, community-driven systems play a pivotal role in shaping the digital landscape. It is essential for stakeholders, developers, and enthusiasts to continue monitoring the advancements in PoW coins and collaborate to overcome challenges and unlock the full potential of these innovative technologies.

Summarizing the Key Takeaways and Lessons Learned

As we reach the conclusion of Book 3, it is essential to summarize the key takeaways and lessons learned from our exploration of Proof-of-Work (PoW) coins. Throughout this journey, we have delved into the unique characteristics, use cases, challenges, and future prospects of Ixcoin, Freicoin, Dogecoin, Vertcoin, and SiaCoin. By distilling the knowledge gained, we can gain valuable insights into the broader implications of PoW coins and their role in the evolution of blockchain technology.

1. Embracing Decentralization and Trustless Systems:

One of the core principles underlying PoW coins is the concept of decentralization. We have learned that decentralization plays a vital role in ensuring network security, preventing censorship, and promoting trustless systems. By distributing power and decision-making authority among participants, PoW coins enable individuals to transact and engage in a peer-to-peer manner without the need for intermediaries. This has significant implications for financial inclusion, privacy, and user autonomy.

2. Balancing Security and Scalability:

Throughout our exploration, we have encountered the challenge of striking a balance between security and scalability. While PoW consensus algorithms provide robust security by requiring computational work to validate transactions, they can also introduce limitations in terms of transaction throughput and energy consumption. Understanding this trade-off is crucial for developers, researchers, and industry stakeholders as they strive to enhance blockchain technology and optimize its performance.

3. Harnessing Community Engagement:

The success of PoW coins is heavily dependent on community engagement. We have witnessed the power of vibrant and passionate communities surrounding these coins, driving innovation, philanthropy, and adoption. Community engagement fosters trust, encourages participation, and creates a sense of ownership among users. It is through the collective efforts of these communities that PoW coins have gained recognition and established themselves as influential players in the cryptocurrency landscape.

4. Exploring Alternative Economic Models:

The exploration of PoW coins has also exposed us to alternative economic models. Coins like Freicoin with demurrage mechanisms challenge traditional notions of money and wealth accumulation. They aim to create more equitable systems by discouraging hoarding and promoting the circulation of currency. These alternative economic models encourage us to question existing financial systems and explore innovative approaches to value exchange and distribution.

5. Addressing Environmental Concerns:

The environmental impact of PoW coins, particularly their energy consumption, has been a topic of discussion and concern. As we move forward, it is crucial to address these environmental challenges and seek sustainable solutions. Innovations such as energy-efficient mining algorithms, the utilization of renewable energy sources, and the exploration of alternative consensus mechanisms can help mitigate the ecological footprint of PoW coins.

6. Collaborative Synergies and Interoperability:

The exploration of PoW coins has highlighted the potential for collaborative synergies and interoperability among blockchain projects. By fostering collaboration and interoperability, we can harness the strengths of different coins and platforms to create more robust and versatile blockchain ecosystems. Interoperability facilitates seamless value transfer, cross-chain functionality, and the integration of various decentralized applications, leading to a more interconnected and efficient blockchain landscape.

7. Nurturing Innovation and Adaptation:

In the ever-evolving world of cryptocurrencies, it is crucial to nurture innovation and adaptation. PoW coins have demonstrated their resilience and ability to adapt to emerging challenges and technological advancements. By fostering an environment that encourages experimentation, research, and development, we can ensure that PoW coins continue to evolve and address the changing needs of users and the industry as a whole.

Conclusion:

In conclusion, our exploration of PoW coins in Book 3 has provided us with valuable insights into the world of decentralized digital currencies. We have learned about the significance of decentralization, the balance between security and scalability, the power of community engagement, the potential for alternative economic models, the need for environmental sustainability, the benefits of collaborative synergies, and the importance of nurturing innovation and adaptation.

As we reflect on the key takeaways and lessons learned, it becomes evident that PoW coins have made significant contributions to the advancement of blockchain technology. They have challenged traditional financial systems, fostered inclusive and participatory economies, and pushed the boundaries of what is possible in the digital realm. However, they also face ongoing challenges and must continue to evolve to remain relevant in a rapidly changing landscape.

Moving forward, it is imperative for stakeholders, developers, and enthusiasts to continue learning, collaborating, and innovating. By leveraging the knowledge gained from the exploration of PoW coins, we can contribute to the advancement of blockchain technology, shape the future of digital economies, and realize the transformative potential of decentralized systems.

Looking Towards the Future: Opportunities and Challenges in the Blockchain Space

As we conclude our exploration of Proof-of-Work (PoW) coins and their impact on the blockchain industry, it is crucial to look towards the future and identify the opportunities and challenges that lie ahead. The evolving landscape of blockchain technology presents immense potential for disruption, innovation, and transformation across various sectors. In this section, we will delve into the exciting opportunities that await, as well as the challenges that must be overcome to realize the full potential of blockchain.

1. Advancing Scalability and Throughput:

Scalability has been a persistent challenge in the blockchain space. As more applications and users join the network, the need for efficient and scalable solutions becomes paramount. Fortunately, technological advancements such as layer-2 protocols, sharding, and off-chain solutions like state channels hold promise in addressing scalability concerns. By improving transaction throughput and reducing latency, these innovations can unlock new possibilities for widespread blockchain adoption.

2. Enhancing Privacy and Security:

Privacy and security have always been vital considerations in the blockchain ecosystem. As blockchain applications continue to permeate various industries, maintaining data privacy and protecting against malicious attacks becomes even more critical. Advancements in zero-knowledge proofs, homomorphic encryption, and privacy-focused protocols can strengthen the privacy features of blockchain networks, enabling individuals and organizations to transact and store data securely.

3. Bridging Traditional and Decentralized Systems:

For blockchain technology to reach its full potential, it is crucial to bridge the gap between traditional systems and decentralized networks. Interoperability protocols and cross-chain solutions can facilitate seamless integration between different blockchains and legacy systems, enabling efficient value transfer and data exchange. This convergence will pave the way for real-world adoption and allow blockchain applications to interact with existing infrastructure seamlessly.

4. Harnessing the Power of Decentralized Finance (DeFi):

Decentralized Finance (DeFi) has emerged as one of the most promising applications of blockchain technology. DeFi protocols enable transparent, permissionless, and programmable financial services, revolutionizing traditional finance. The future of blockchain will see the continued growth of DeFi, with opportunities for lending, borrowing, decentralized exchanges, stablecoins, and more. However, it also presents challenges such as regulatory compliance, scalability, and security, which need to be addressed for sustainable growth.

5. Exploring the Intersection of Blockchain and Internet of Things (IoT):

The convergence of blockchain technology and the Internet of Things (IoT) holds immense potential for transforming industries such as supply chain management, healthcare, energy, and more. Blockchain can provide trust, transparency, and security in IoT ecosystems, enabling seamless data sharing, automated transactions, and efficient device management. However, the integration of blockchain and IoT also requires addressing scalability, interoperability, and data privacy concerns.

6. Overcoming Regulatory and Legal Hurdles:

As blockchain technology continues to disrupt traditional industries, regulatory and legal challenges arise. Governments and regulatory bodies are grappling with developing frameworks that foster innovation while ensuring consumer protection, data privacy, and financial stability.

Striking the right balance between regulation and innovation will be crucial in shaping the future of blockchain and allowing its potential to be fully realized.

7. Fostering Education and Awareness:

Education and awareness are fundamental in driving blockchain adoption and understanding its implications. As the technology becomes more complex, it is essential to empower individuals, businesses, and policymakers with the knowledge needed to make informed decisions. Initiatives focusing on education, research, and collaboration can help demystify blockchain, increase awareness, and promote responsible adoption across diverse sectors.

In conclusion, the future of blockchain holds vast opportunities for innovation, disruption, and societal transformation. Advancements in scalability, privacy, interoperability, DeFi, IoT integration, and regulatory frameworks will shape the trajectory of blockchain technology. However, challenges related to scalability, security, regulation, and education must be addressed to unlock the full potential of blockchain.

As we move forward, it is crucial for stakeholders, industry leaders, policymakers, and the wider community to collaborate and drive the evolution of blockchain technology. By fostering innovation, addressing challenges, and leveraging the transformative power of blockchain, we can create a future where decentralized systems redefine trust, enable inclusive economies, and empower individuals on a global scale. The journey ahead is both exciting and challenging, but the potential rewards make it a path worth pursuing.

THE END

To help you better understand the language and concepts related to aging and older adults, below you will find a list of key terms and their definitions.

1. Proof-of-Work (PoW): A consensus mechanism used in blockchain networks where participants must solve computationally intensive puzzles to validate and add new blocks to the blockchain. It requires significant computational power and helps maintain the security and integrity of the network.

2. Blockchain: A decentralized and distributed ledger that records transactions across multiple computers or nodes. Each transaction is verified and added to a block, which is then linked to previous blocks, creating an immutable chain of transactions.

3. Decentralization: The distribution of power and control across a network of participants, eliminating the need for a central authority. In the context of blockchain, decentralization refers to the absence of a single governing entity and the democratic decision-making process among network participants.

4. Cryptocurrency: A digital or virtual currency that uses cryptography for security and operates independently of

a central bank. Cryptocurrencies, such as Bitcoin, are typically built on blockchain technology.

5. Scalability: The ability of a system to handle an increasing amount of transactions or users without compromising performance. In the context of blockchain, scalability refers to the capacity of a blockchain network to process a large number of transactions efficiently.

6. Privacy: The protection of sensitive information and the ability to control access to personal data. In the context of blockchain, privacy refers to the measures taken to ensure that transaction details and user identities are not publicly visible.

7. Security: The protection of blockchain networks and transactions against unauthorized access, fraud, and malicious attacks. It involves implementing cryptographic algorithms, secure key management, and robust consensus mechanisms to maintain the integrity of the blockchain.

8. Interoperability: The ability of different blockchain networks or systems to communicate, exchange data, and interact seamlessly. Interoperability aims to facilitate the flow of information and value between disparate blockchain platforms.

9. Decentralized Finance (DeFi): A financial ecosystem built on blockchain technology that aims to

provide open and inclusive financial services, including lending, borrowing, trading, and asset management, without the need for traditional intermediaries.

10. Internet of Things (IoT): A network of interconnected physical devices, vehicles, buildings, and other objects that are embedded with sensors, software, and network connectivity. The integration of blockchain with IoT enables secure and trusted data exchange and automated transactions.

11. Regulatory Compliance: Adherence to laws, regulations, and guidelines set by governments and regulatory bodies. In the context of blockchain, regulatory compliance involves ensuring that blockchain-based systems and applications comply with relevant legal and regulatory requirements.

12. Education and Awareness: Initiatives aimed at providing knowledge and understanding of blockchain technology to individuals, businesses, policymakers, and the general public. Education and awareness programs play a crucial role in fostering responsible blockchain adoption and driving innovation.

13. Innovation: The development and implementation of new ideas, technologies, and approaches that bring about positive change. In the context of blockchain, innovation

refers to the continuous evolution and improvement of blockchain technology and its applications.

14. Transformation: The profound changes and disruptions that occur as a result of the adoption and integration of blockchain technology. Blockchain has the potential to transform various industries, business models, and societal structures by redefining trust, transparency, and value exchange.

Supporting Materials

Introduction:

Nakamoto, S. (2008). Bitcoin: A peer-to-peer electronic cash system. Retrieved from https://bitcoin.org/bitcoin.pdf

Chapter 1: Ixcoin (IXC), established 2011 - "Global decentralized currency."

Ixcoin. (n.d.). Retrieved from https://ixcoin.net/

Ixcoin (IXC) on CoinMarketCap. (n.d.). Retrieved from https://coinmarketcap.com/currencies/ixcoin/

Chapter 2: Freicoin (FRC), established 2012 - "Demurrage currency with distribution mechanisms."

Freicoin. (n.d.). Retrieved from https://freico.in/

Freicoin (FRC) on CoinMarketCap. (n.d.). Retrieved from https://coinmarketcap.com/currencies/freicoin/

Chapter 3: Dogecoin (DOGE), established 2013 - "The fun and friendly internet currency."

Dogecoin. (n.d.). Retrieved from https://dogecoin.com/

Dogecoin (DOGE) on CoinMarketCap. (n.d.). Retrieved from https://coinmarketcap.com/currencies/dogecoin/

Chapter 4: Vertcoin (VTC), established 2014 - "Peer-to-peer digital currency with ASIC resistance."

Vertcoin. (n.d.). Retrieved from https://vertcoin.org/

Vertcoin (VTC) on CoinMarketCap. (n.d.). Retrieved from https://coinmarketcap.com/currencies/vertcoin/

Chapter 5: SiaCoin (SC), established 2015 - "Decentralized cloud storage platform."

Sia. (n.d.). Retrieved from https://sia.tech/

SiaCoin (SC) on CoinMarketCap. (n.d.). Retrieved from https://coinmarketcap.com/currencies/siacoin/

Chapter 6: Comparative Analysis and Synergies

Buterin, V. (2014). A next-generation smart contract and decentralized application platform. Retrieved from https://ethereum.org/whitepaper/

Wood, G. (2014). Ethereum: A secure decentralised generalised transaction ledger. Retrieved from https://ethereum.org/pdfs/EthereumYellowPaper.pdf

Chapter 7: Shaping the Future of Blockchain

Tapscott, D., & Tapscott, A. (2016). Blockchain revolution: How the technology behind bitcoin is changing money, business, and the world. Penguin.

Swan, M. (2015). Blockchain: Blueprint for a new economy. O'Reilly Media.

Conclusion:

Antonopoulos, A. M. (2017). Mastering Bitcoin: Unlocking digital cryptocurrencies. O'Reilly Media.

Tapscott, D., & Tapscott, A. (2016). Blockchain revolution: How the technology behind bitcoin is changing money, business, and the world. Penguin.